BERK
FOLK
TALES

BERKSHIRE
FOLK TALES

DAVID ENGLAND
& TINA BILBÉ

ILLUSTRATED BY
SUE WHITE

The
History
Press

We dedicate this book to all those generations of Berkshire local historians and librarians who have collected and preserved these stories.

First published 2013

The History Press
The Mill, Brimscombe Port
Stroud, Gloucestershire, GL5 2QG
www.thehistorypress.co.uk

British Library Cataloguing in Publication Data.
A catalogue record for this book is available from the British Library.

ISBN 978 0 7524 6745 0

Typesetting and origination by The History Press
Printed in Great Britain

CONTENTS

FOREWORD

Within these pages are the voices of folk and the firesides of centuries; the dust of ages gathered from castle, keep and cottage, transported by eye, ear and mind, polished with age and retelling, cut to shape and breathed on by succeeding generations.

This collection of traditional stories from the Royal County of Berkshire is set to indulge, intrigue and dazzle the imagination. Time on these pages stands still and centuries stand in suspension; yesterday and today merge as you, the reader, take up the telling.

Del Reid, 2013
The Society for Storytelling
Coordinator for National Storytelling Week

PREFACE

It is the summer of 1899. A group of antiquaries set out from Reading on a tour of Berkshire in a wagonette. At each town or village on their itinerary, they, or the locals they meet on their journey, tell their favourite Berkshire folk tales. The route the antiquaries take is described in the text, so that you too can make the journey and tell the tales.

In 1909 Miss L. Salmon wrote about 'Untravelled Berkshire' in her delightful book of the same name. Indeed, much of the old county remains untravelled, with its varied landscapes, picturesque villages and historic inns; its churches and churchyards superimposed on ancient sacred sites, all accessible via quiet, winding lanes. Our book is a gazetteer to help you discover this land and its stories.

The antiquaries have differing voices, and this is reflected in their tales. As an illustration of this, compare the three stories based in the Vale of White Horse: White Horse Revels, King Gaarge and the Dragon, and Wayland the Smith.

Researching the sources of Berkshire folk tales has been an essential element in writing this book, as is shown by our extensive bibliography. Sometimes, a folk tale consists of unconnected fragments. Then, as storytellers, we have the intuitive task of making connections and weaving a convincing tale, with characterisation and drama. At other times, we are faced with an unwieldy, incoherent mass of source data. Then, as storytellers, we have the task of picking out the essential elements and presenting them as a coherent story. Thus, we have sought to write entertaining tales whilst remaining faithful to our sources. In so doing, where we felt it was necessary, we have recorded the bare bones of a story, as we received it, below our tale.

We hope you enjoy travelling with the antiquaries on your Berkshire folk tales journey.

David England and Tina Bilbé, 2013

ONE

READING

MY RECORD OF A TRIP THROUGH BERKSHIRE IN THE SUMMER OF 1899 - BY LOUISE FIELDGATE

It was the beginning of 1899; the last year of the nineteenth century and fast approaching a new millennium. My brother, David, had taken up an interest in folklore and was voicing concerns that the old tales would soon be lost as more and more people learned to read and moved into the towns. Thus was born the idea for a trip during the summer vacation, with a group of antiquarian acquaintances who my brother had been in correspondence with over the last year or so. We would research what tales had already been collected, enquire about possible contacts to meet on our journey, and travel the length and breadth of the county retelling the tales we had collected. We would meet our contacts to hear more along the way, and explore the land-scape from which the stories had arisen. 'A motley crew in a ship of fools', our uncle called us, but what did we care for that.

It was agreed that we should gather in Reading, where the Great Western and the South Eastern railways meet. Rooms were booked at the Great Western Hotel, opposite the station, and on the appointed day our happy band assembled: Professor James Gaunt, Revd John Plumb, Cecil Vanderpump, Mrs Arabella Trump, William Beauchamp Esq., Dr Harold Benjamin, Joseph Cleave, Henry Rowland, David and me.

Berkshire's ancient county town is situated a short distance from the south bank of the Thames, and a little upstream of its junction

with the Kennet. It is linked to the Severn via the Kennet & Avon
Canal and is 39 miles from London along the Great West Road.
Reading is the commercial centre of a thriving agricultural district;
it has extensive breweries, iron foundries, and agricultural imple-
ment and engineering works. Boats are built by the riverside and
there are brick, tile and pottery works nearby. The two industries,
however, for which the town is famous throughout the world, are
the great biscuit works of Messrs Huntley & Palmers, and the seed
establishment of Messrs Sutton & Sons.

The town has a long history and was first recorded in 868.
But it was the founding of Reading Abbey that increased the
importance of the town immeasurably. In medieval times,
Reading was famous for producing fine woollen cloth. One
notable worthy of the town was 'Old King Cole', whose wagons
of cloth held up the King for so long that his anger turned to the
realisation of how useful an ally the wealthy Thomas Cole would
be. The result of their meeting, so the story goes, was the crea-
tion of a standard measure for cloth throughout England. But a
gruesome fate awaited Thomas, as our good friend and colleague
Dr Benjamin related:

The Pleasant History of Thomas of Reading

Hundreds of years ago, the Hospice of Colebrook provided refuge
and hospitality to passing pilgrims visiting Windsor. Locals called
it the 'Ospice, the name corrupting over the centuries to become
the Osbridge Inn. Thanks to English explorers, word of Africa's
curious and exotic creatures inspired another change of name: it
became the Ostrich Inn.

The landlord's name was Jarman, and he and his wife ran a
thriving tavern. Wealthy merchants would stop over at the Ostrich
for a comfortable night's lodging, good ale and a feast of scrump-
tious penny pork pasties. One such merchant was Thomas Cole,
a rich and successful clothier from Reading. As he rode down from
London, his mouth watered at the prospect of those penny pasties,
richly filled with roasted pork and spices, and oozing with thick
pork gravy.

On arrival at the Ostrich, Thomas quickly stabled his horse, handed over his purse (fat from his London trade) to Jarman's wife for safe keeping, and put in his order for penny pork pasties.

'Oi put 'e in moi bes' room, zur, above moi warm kitchen,' said Jarman's wife. 'Youm be warm as pork crackling.'

Later, sated on good ale and pork pasties, Thomas retired to the Jarmans' best room.

Unbeknown to the patrons of the Ostrich, there was a dark side to the Jarmans' business. It had been the wife's idea to make the floor of the best room pivot on an iron beam, with the floor held in place by two stout iron pins, and it was Jarman who had crafted it. The bed was bolted to the pivoted floor, positioned over a mighty cauldron used to seethe the liquor for brewing.

The moonless night was deepest dark. Nearby, a screech owl uttered a piteous cry. A raven, blacker than the night, croaked by the bedroom window. Thomas Cole was oblivious to these dire warnings and snored on. The Jarmans listened at the door until Thomas' snoring fell into a steady rhythm. Then they tiptoed down to the kitchen.

Jarman quietly slipped out the two iron pins. Slowly, oh so slowly, the finely balanced best-bedroom floor, with the bed upon it, tipped the still sleeping Thomas of Reading – like a burial at sea into the foaming deep – into the hot foaming oil in the cauldron beneath.

Jarman and his wife swiftly hauled Thomas out of the cauldron with grappling hooks, a look of faint surprise still lingering upon his deep-fried features. He was quickly quartered, placed in roast-ing pans, and popped into the large pre-heated oven.

By the time Thomas was done to a turn, Jarman and his wife had mixed and rolled out the pastry and laid out the butcher's choppers and knives. This was the part they loved the best, chopping up the roast meat and slicing it into chunks to make their delicious penny pork pasties, which were so good that even the Ostrich Inn's own cellarmen and serving wenches relished them. The Jarmans split open Thomas' bones and made rich marrow gravy to moisten the meat. Finally, they sealed the pasties with a little milk, cut two holes in the pastry tops to let the steam release, and put the pasties in the oven to cook.

When all was done, and the pasties were left to cool for the day's trade, the Jarmans retired to their beds, content in the knowledge that they were made richer by the contents of Thomas' purse and the value of his horse and flesh.

Jarman was roused from his contented slumber by a furious beating on the inn door. Glancing out of the window, he saw two men with Thomas' horse in the yard. Thinking his wicked deeds had been discovered, Jarman made off into Windsor Forest, leav-ing his wife to be apprehended by the constable. Jarman didn't get far. A search party was swiftly formed, their hunting dogs quickly picked up his scent, and Jarman was caught hiding in a tree.

At Thomas' home in Reading, his wife had become anxious, as she had expected him home that night. She feared he had been set upon by the notorious highwayman, Dick Turpin, who preyed on travellers in Maidenhead Thicket. So, she had sent a servant by horse to find him and bring him home. The servant had ridden through Maidenhead Thicket and over Maidenhead Bridge all the way to Colnbrook without finding his master.

Meanwhile, Thomas' horse had escaped from the stable and discovered a mare in a field close by. The horse was in the act of enthusiastically tupping the equally enthusiastic mare when the mare's owner found them. Disgruntled by the liberties taken with his mare, the owner was leading the horse to the Ostrich, to enquire of its owner, when he met Thomas' servant, who recognised the horse as his master's.

With so much evidence of Thomas' presence at the Ostrich – his horse, fat purse, and clothes – Jarman gave up any pretence of innocence and made a full confession. Except, thumbing at his wife, he said, ''Twere all 'er idea, I just fixed t' floor.'

It did no good; both Jarman and his wife got a hanging. It turned out that sixty of the Jarmans' guests had been turned into penny pork pasties at the Ostrich Inn.

Sources

Deloney, Thomas, *The History of Thomas of Reading*, 1632

Westwood, Jennifer and Simpson, Jacqueline, *The Lore of the Land*, 2006

This story has been given here its original, rather curious, title, *c.* 1598.

You can visit the Ostrich Inn at Colnbrook. It is the third oldest pub in the UK, dating from 1106. It has exposed beams, ancient fireplaces, crooked stairs, and a cobbled courtyard.

TWO

SONNING

After a good breakfast and our first story, we piled onto the wagonette, drawn by two spritely horses. We made our way past the Forbury Gardens and Reading Gaol – a smart brick castle erected in 1883 with capacity for 224 prisoners, and made notorious in the ballad by Oscar Wilde. Crossing a backwater, we turned left and passed Huntley & Palmers' biscuit manufactory, smelling the wonderful aroma of baking as we crossed the main channel of the Kennet, and joined the Great West Road eastwards, following the tramlines past noble houses up to Cemetery Junction. A little further on we passed under the railway line and our sense of smell was again delighted, this time by the profusion of flowers in Sutton's Seeds trial ground. Up Shepherds Hill, the town far behind us now, we crossed over the railway line and turned left into Sonning Lane.

We stopped the wagonette just before we reached the gates of Holme Park, and explored the pleasant, picturesque village on foot. Walking past a cottage named Turpins, reputed to have belonged to Dick Turpin's aunt, we entered the churchyard. The grey church tower and spacious thirteenth-century flint and stone building, once the seat of a bishopric, contains a wealth of interesting brasses, tombs and monuments. The river below the church is crossed by an ancient brick bridge of eleven arches, with beautiful views up and down the Thames.

Returning through the churchyard, we passed the Bull public house and walked up the High Street. We turned left, passed by the almshouses, and stopped outside the new parish hall, built on or near the site of an old alehouse named the Dog, a fitting place to rest and hear Joseph Cleave tell our next tale, about Berkshire highwaymen.

BERKSHIRE HIGHWAYMEN

The lonely heaths and thickets of Berkshire, crossed by main highways, were a great refuge for felons of every kind – highwaymen, robbers, footpads, outlaws and murderers. The isolated Hind's Head Inn, in the middle of Bagshot Heath, was a favourite haunt for these villains.

Sonning: Black Bess or Knight of The Road[1]

The most famous, or infamous, of Berkshire's felons were Dick Turpin and Claude Du Vall.

From an early age, Dick Turpin knew the kind of career he wanted: 'One which stands to deliver me handsome returns, is adventurous and fun, with just a spice of danger, demands little effort on my part, and leaves me plenty of time for carousing.'

One day, his path in life became clear. 'I know!' he exclaimed, 'I shall be a highwayman. It will give me all I ever wanted.' He laughed aloud at his next thought, 'And my byword shall be 'Stand and Deliver', as I relieve my patrons of their valuables.'

Dick realised this was a good choice. It required little outlay to become an outlaw, just a decent pair of pistols, a black mask, and a strong horse with plenty of intelligence. To get started in his new profession, he would need to steal a horse. So he did.

Growing up in Hempstead, Essex, not too far from the Great North Road, Dick decided to ply his trade on the quieter and lonelier stretches of this major coach route between London and York. Soon he was able to buy his dream horse from a gypsy site at Tinkler Leas near Pontefract Lane, Leeds. He called her Black Bess. She was so strong, feisty and fast that an affinity formed between Bess and Dick straightaway.

Dick's mother had a sister who had a pub at Sonning in Berkshire, the Dog Inn. So when things got a bit too hot for him up the Great North Road, he decided to visit her. His aunt not only made him welcome, she actually applauded his choice of career, enjoyed the tales of his exploits, and suggested a few refinements. There was a stall below the Dog Inn where Black Bess could be hidden, and there was an easy escape route into Oxfordshire over Sonning Bridge. Moreover, in Maidenhead Thicket and on Bagshot Heath, 'Stand and Deliver' could yield rich pickings.

In Berkshire, Dick's trade offered him fun, adventure and excitement, but little danger. The manors of Sonning, Bray and Bagshot had each a single constable, unpaid and appointed for only a year. It was the constable's job to raise the hue and cry in order to arrest and detain criminals, but first it was up to the victims to identify the culprits – and unmasking a masked highwayman was not easy.

Dick's plan was to develop a network of safe houses, mostly inns, where, if the hue and cry was raised, he could hide after a hold-up, enjoying flagons of fine ale before escaping when the coast was clear.

There was his aunt's Dog Inn, where Dick could hide while Black Bess trotted down the ramp into her underground stall. When the hue and cry had passed, he could escape over Sonning Bridge into Oxfordshire, beyond the constable's jurisdiction.

At the George Inn at Wallingford, Dick slept in a room overlooking the entrance arch, where Black Bess was tethered. When cornered, he could leap from the window onto Bess's back and gallop to safety.

The remote Hind's Head Inn was an ideal safe house for Dick's forays on Bagshot Heath, as it had a secret passageway large enough for Dick and Bess to gallop through.

Dick's favourite resort after a hold-up was an Elizabethan farmhouse at Twyford, where Black Bess could hide herself among other horses, in the field behind the house. The farmhouse had a byre on its ground floor, with outside stone steps up to living quarters warmed by the heat of the animals beneath. Here, he was always made welcome, and given a comfortable room overlooking the road. In a beam in this room was a secret hollow, which Dick used to hide his stolen jewels.

Dick Turpin made regular visits to his old haunts on the Great North Road, and reached an ignominious end – the end of a hangman's rope – in York, having been found guilty of stealing a horse.

The Wokingham 'Blacks'

The most notorious band of outlaws were the Wokingham 'Blacks', who blackened their faces so as not to be identified. Under the leadership of a farm labourer, Will Shorter, the 'Blacks' became a dangerous gang of criminals, terrorising the neighbourhood, robbing, poaching, blackmailing, and committing murder.

Partly through intimidation, and partly because their blackened faces prevented them from being recognised, the gang escaped punishment. However, they were so feared that a special Act of Parliament was passed, called the 'Black Act', which made it a felony to blacken one's face.

Several members of the gang were finally killed on Bagshot Heath, trying to evade capture, while others, including Will Shorter, were transported.

Bracknell: Claude Du Vall

Claude Du Vall was born in France, the son of a miller. At the age of fourteen, due to his willingness to run errands and undertake the meanest of tasks, he inveigled himself into the services of some English gentlemen, living in lodgings in the Faubourg St Germain, which were something between an alehouse and a bawdy-house. He continued in this service until he was able to sail to England, on a wave of enthusiasm for the restoration of King Charles II, as footman to the Duke of Richmond.

Claude thrived on the extravagances of restoration London, becoming proficient at gambling, drunkenness and philandering. His position as footman, though lowly, brought him into contact with young ladies of quality. Whenever he found a young lady married to an aged or neglectful husband, Claude's dashing good looks, confident French manners, and silver, persuasive tongue soon drew her into a surreptitious and delightful dalliance.

It was plain to him, however, that in order to maintain his lifestyle he needed a more lucrative profession than that of footman – one which furnished him with maximum income for minimum effort, and left plenty of time for debauchery. So, Claude became a highwayman. A few days spent around Bracknell Forest and Bagshot Heath, he soon found, could set him up in London for the rest of the month. Lodging at the Hind's Head Inn on Bagshot Heath, too, had its compensations: gambling, debauchery and good company.

Even as a highwayman, Claude's gallantry towards ladies of quality did not desert him. He received intelligence one day of a knight travelling across Bagshot Heath in his coach with 400s in his purse. When Claude stopped the coach and demanded that the knight hand over the purse, the knight's spritely lady, with enormous presence of mind, took out her flageolet and played a brisk tune. As playing the flageolet was one of Claude's own accomplishments, he took out his own instrument and played with her.

Then he addressed the knight. 'Monsieur, your lady plays excellently, and I have no doubt but she dances just as well. Will it please you for her to step from the coach and dance one courante with me upon the heath?'

'I dare not deny anything, sir,' the knight replied readily, 'to a gentleman of such quality and good manners.'

Claude leapt lightly from his horse and helped the lady down from the coach. Then, Claude and the lady danced a courante upon the grass with all the grace and elegance you might find in a ballroom at Versailles.

When the dance was done, Claude handed the lady into the coach before addressing the knight. 'Monsieur, it may have escaped your notice, but you have not paid for the entertainment.'

The knight opened his purse, looked Claude in the eye, and with a smile handed over 100*s*. Claude received this with good grace and a courteous response. 'Monsieur, 100 shillings freely given is better than ten times the amount taken by force, and by your generosity in allowing me to dance and play with your lady, you are excused the 300 shillings remaining in your purse. Monsieur et Madame, I wish you bon voyage.'

Claude then allowed the coach to continue on its way, and the knight and his lady passed safely across the heath.

Alas, Claude's career was all too brief. He was such a terror to travellers that large rewards were offered, and he was captured, while drunk, in the Hole-in-the-Wall Tavern in Chandos Street, and condemned to death. It was hardly surprising how many ladies of quality interceded on his behalf, but the King expressly denied him all hope of pardon, and he was hanged at Tyburn at the age of twenty-seven. His body was cut down and laid in state at the Tangier Tavern, St Giles, where those great ladies sobbed bitter tears over him.

He was buried in the centre aisle of St Paul's Church, Covent Garden, under a stone inscribed with his epitaph:

Here lies Du Vall
Reader, if male thou art, look to thy purse
If female, to thy heart

❧

After this story, the wagonette collected us from outside Sonning Village Hall. We trundled on to the end of the road and turned right onto Charvil Lane; we crossed the Great West Road and carried on to Twyford, where Mr Cleave pointed out the old farm-house mentioned in his tale.

SOURCES

Heelas, Arthur T., *Historical Sketch of Wokingham*, 1930
Lee, Sidney (Ed.), *Dictionary of National Biography*, Vol. LVII, 1899
Stephen, Leslie (Ed.), *Dictionary of National Biography*, Vol. XVI, 1888
Viles, Edward, *Black Bess or the Knight of the Road*, 1866

જી

Two hundred and fifty years after Dick Turpin, the author had an office in the old farmhouse where Dick Turpin had slept. Alas, the hollow beam contained no jewels. You will find the beautiful Elizabethan building on Twyford High Street.

Claude Du Vall's burial in St Paul's Church, Covent Garden, known as 'The Actor's Church', is a folk tale.

THREE

WARGRAVE

At the crossroads a short distance further along the road, we turned left past a few good houses and some farmland, before crossing the Great West Road again as we made our way to Wargrave. By this time we were in need of refreshment of a more bodily nature, and stopped for coffee at the Bull Hotel. This building is said to be haunted by the unfaithful wife of a former landlord, who, on discovering her infidelity, ordered her to leave house, husband and child. Here Revd Plumb told us the story of Queen Emma, who is said to have had a palace here.

Queen Emma's Ordeal by Fire

Cnut, son of Sweyn Forkbeard, once King of Denmark, Norway and England, invaded the land. At first, King Æthelred and Queen Emma held out in London against Cnut's offensive. Within the year, however, Æthelred was dead and Emma was holding out alone against the forces of Cnut.

Power, politics, passion and piety characterised the turbulent life of Emma of Normandy, twice Queen Consort and mother of two kings of England.

Queen Emma was the second wife of King Æthelred. Though she had been made to use the name of King Æthelred's first wife, Ælfgifu, on formal occasions, in the bargain she struck with Æthelred this humiliation was weightily counterbalanced by receiving extensive lands which had belonged to King Æthelred's mother, Queen Ælfthryth. Queen Emma continued Queen Ælfthryth's pious practice of largesse towards the clergy and religious houses.

When Cnut went to parley with Emma for a kingdom, expecting her to plead for life and liberty for herself and her sons, he came away with more than he had bargained for. He gained not only the kingdom of England but also a passionate wife and powerful political ally.

When Emma went to parley with Cnut, she had in mind an inventive twist to her fortunes: to swap the cockpit of conflict for the marriage bed. She employed all her passionate allure and political guile to seduce her adversary, thereby retaining her political power, securing the safety of her sons, and acquiring a worthy lover to share her bed. The love match between Cnut the Great and Queen Emma lasted nearly twenty years until Cnut's death, and they had one son, Cnut's heir Harthacnut.

When Cnut the Great died, Harold Harefoot, Cnut's illegitimate son by his former 'handfast' wife, seized the kingdom while Harthacnut was busy fighting in Scandinavia. Emma's sons, Edward and Alfred, escaped to Normandy and Emma took refuge in Bruges with the Count of Flanders, where she commissioned a treatise 'In Praise of Queen Emma'.[2]

Back at the English court, Harold Harefoot had died, and though Harthacnut had been declared king and Edward had been sworn in as his heir, Harthacnut's grip on power remained fragile. By circulating 'In Praise of Queen Emma', Emma sought to garner political support for her sons and herself – successfully, as it turned out – by shamelessly and cleverly presenting history in a way which placed Cnut, herself and her sons in the best possible light.[3]

A surprising woman, when Harthacnut died she supported Magnus, King of Norway and Denmark, rather than her son Edward. We can only speculate why she favoured, over her own blood, a sixteen-year-old lad with light blond hair, regular features and light complexion, who was quick-witted, generous and a brave warrior. For once her machinations failed, and Edward, later Edward the Confessor, became King of England.

Whatever Emma's reason for favouring Magnus, it strained her relationship with her son and left her in disgrace in the eyes of his court. With restored perspicacity, she chose to make her home at her manor in the Berkshire village of Wargrave. This avoided embarrassment to her son, by creating some distance from his court. At the same time, it allowed her reasonable access to him in London or Winchester via the old London-Silchester-Winchester road. Despite his ambivalence towards her as his mother, she knew the King still valued her political insights. She also knew he was malleable, and in this way she could retain her political influence.

This is the quality of the woman – determined, inventive, surprising, and with a passionate nature – who was to face an ordeal by fire at the behest of Robert, Archbishop of Canterbury.

Robert was a Norman. He had been Abbot of Jumièges, and had met and befriended Edward in his long exile in Normandy during Cnut's reign. He had accompanied Edward on his return to England to become king and was one of Edward's closest advisors. Robert was also ruthlessly ambitious; his crowning achievement to date was having Edward appoint him as Archbishop of Canterbury, despite the cathedral chapter's election of a different candidate. Robert bitterly resented any other influence on the King, and had driven another close advisor, Lord Godwin, into exile by accusing him of plotting to kill Edward.

For Robert, therefore, the influence of King Edward's mother, Queen Emma, could not be tolerated. Moreover, this fastidious, celibate monk felt a profound distaste for women in general, and for this woman in particular, for her worldliness and flamboyant allure.

She had to go. But how was he to persuade the King to get rid of his own mother? Her support for Magnus was not sufficient to indict her, for she had otherwise been fully supportive of her son throughout his life, but it gave him a clue to her downfall: her passionate nature would destroy her.

Robert advised the King, 'I deeply regret to tell thee, Sire, that Ælfwine, Bishop of Winchester, until his death three years ago, was overly intimate with thy mother, Queen Emma. As Archbishop of Canterbury, it is my holy duty to ask thee to have Queen Emma prove her innocence, and also, as Ælfwine is no longer here to prove himself, she must prove his innocence at the same time. I am deeply saddened, Sire, to have to bring these tidings.'

Thus did Robert seek to persuade the King to subject his mother to an ordeal by fire.

The King ordered Emma's lands and property to be confiscated and she was sent to a nunnery, Wherwell Abbey. Reflecting on this sudden reversal of her fortunes, Emma realised how, by isolating her malleable son, Robert was a threat not only to her but also to the King and his kingdom. In her response to this threat, Emma's political acumen, passion, and capacity to surprise was to attain a new level.

Emma appealed to bishops whom she trusted for support. When the bishops rallied to support Emma, it pushed Robert into risking stronger language in the presence of the King. 'She is a wild thing, not a woman. She called her slimy lover Christ the Lord.' And worse words he uttered against her, until the King consented to the ordeal by fire.

Though his face remained impassive, Robert was satisfied, and he even felt a little pleasure in his shrivelled heart at having trounced his rival, Queen Emma, so easily.

For the ordeal by fire, Queen Emma was to walk over nine ploughshares that had been heated in the fire until they were red hot. These were placed on the pavement of Winchester Cathedral. As Robert dictated, four ploughshares were to prove her innocence and five were to prove the innocence of Bishop Ælfwine: a double purgation. If Queen Emma was able to walk over all nine red-hot ploughshares unscathed, then her innocence and that of Ælfwine would be proved, but if her feet were burned then she would be considered guilty and condemned to death.

Queen Emma spent the night before her ordeal in prayer to St Swithun, who had been Bishop of Winchester in the time of King Ælfred the Great, and was renowned for having overseen the rebuilding of Winchester's East Gate Bridge over the River Itchen. When visiting the bridge to review the work, St Swithun had met a poor woman who was in great distress, having dropped and broken her basket of eggs. He lightly plucked the basket from the ground and handed it back to her with his blessing, then carried on with his work. When she looked in the basket, to her joy the eggs had all been made whole.

As Queen Emma prayed, she brought this miracle to mind and held St Swithun in her heart with such pious fervour that the saint came to her, saying, 'I am Swithun whom thou hast invoked. Fear not, the fire shall do thee no hurt.'

Early the next morning, a fire was lit in the nave of Winchester's cathedral church of St Swithun, and the nine ploughshares were placed in the fire until they were red hot. King Edward the Confessor and his whole court were assembled, along with the cathedral clergy and Archbishop Robert.

Queen Emma entered the cathedral blindfolded, led by the Bishop of Winchester. With the reassuring words of the cathedral's patron saint in her heart, she uttered an invocation: 'Oh God, who didst save Susannah from the malice of the wicked elders, save me, I humbly entreat thee.'

Led by the bishop, she tripped lightly across the pavement of the nave, so lightly she felt that if she were walking upon eggs they would not break beneath her feet. Turning to the bishop, she asked, 'When shall we come to the ploughshares?'

'Why, ma'am,' he replied in humble amazement, falling upon his knees before her, 'By St Swithun, thou hast stepped upon them already and thou art unharmed. This miracle proves thine innocence and that of the blessed Ælfwine.'

King Edward the Confessor was mortified at having subjected his mother to such a cruel and humiliating torment, and, in that moment, contemplating her demeanour throughout this ordeal, he felt, saw and appreciated her qualities for the very first time. He cast himself at her feet in repentance and pleaded for her forgiveness. He threw off his robes, tore off his shirt to expose his back to the lash, and submitted to atoning stripes from Queen Emma and the Bishop of Winchester. Emma's lands and property were restored.

In gratitude to St Swithun for her deliverance, Queen Emma gave nine of her manors, one for each ploughshare, to the See of Winchester. One of these was her manor of Wargrave.

Robert had overreached himself. By her self-control and calm demeanour, Emma had exposed Robert's overweening and ruthless ambition. He was deposed from his archbishopric at a royal council, stripped of all his personal property, declared an outlaw, and banished to Normandy, where he died soon afterwards, a broken man.

❧

Before we left Wargrave, we stretched our legs and explored this interesting village. Unfortunately, the splendid theatre built by 'Hellgate' Barrymore, who died at the age of twenty-four after a riotous life in the 1790s, no longer exists. I walked down to the church with Revd Plumb and, while admiring the early Norman architecture, the local vicar came up for a chat and told us of plans for a new village hall. The architect's designs for 'Wycliffe Hall' were very stylish and modern, and it was all being paid for by a local woman in memory of her late husband.

Mr Vanderpump and Mr Beauchamp walked up to a riverside hostelry, the George and Dragon, and returned with a sad tale regarding the drowning of the lock-keeper's daughter about twenty years ago.

SOURCE

Gray, Rosemary (Ed.), *The Book of Wargrave, c.* 1986

❧

According to Berkshire folklore, Queen Emma lived for part of her life in Wargrave, survived an ordeal by fire at Winchester after being accused by Archbishop Robert of infidelity with the deceased Bishop Ælfwine, and in gratitude to St Swithun gave her Wargrave manor, along with eight more, to the See of Winchester.

The historical aspects of the story are generally accurate, though not without the storyteller's interpretational flourish.

❧

FOUR

MAIDENHEAD

Back on the wagonette, we went up School Road to rejoin the Great West Road at Hare Hatch, where we turned left towards Maidenhead. At Knowle Hill we passed an ancient hostelry, the Bird in Hand, parts of which are said to be 500 years old. A little further along, on the opposite side of the road, is a beautiful, ivy-clad, red-brick church with its impressive spire built in 1840. Crossing Maidenhead Thicket, our thoughts turned again to highwaymen, as the Revd Plumb informed us that the area had been so infested with them once that the local vicar had been given an extra stipend to cover his losses while working in the parish.

Coming down Castle Hill into Maidenhead, we passed a neat stone church of the Countess of Huntingdon's Connexion, where we crossed the Cookham road and started down High Street. We paused in front of the site of the Greyhound, where King Charles I bade farewell to his children in July 1647. The people of the town are said to have decked the King's route with green boughs and flowers. At the bottom of High Street, we stopped at the Bear for lunch, and the landlord regaled us with tales about the Vicar of Bray, including a droll story of his lunch with King James at that very hostelry.

The Vicar of Bray and the Windsor Martyrs

There is a famous Vicar of Bray, Simon Alleyn, who kept his living during five reigns – King Henry VIII, King Edward VI, Queen Jane, Queen Mary I, and Queen Elizabeth I – despite frequent shifts in the religious convictions and ordinances of Protestant and Catholic kings and queens.

As a young cleric, Simon Alleyn had witnessed the execution of the Windsor Martyrs for flouting the 'Act of Six Articles'[4], which asserted King Henry VIII's Catholic beliefs.

The Windsor Martyrs consisted of three men: a priest, Anthony Pierson, who preached against the Six Articles; a churchwarden, Henry Filmer, in whose home writings against the Six Articles were found; and Robert Testwood, a chorister at St George's Chapel, who was heard to make vituperative comments to the effect that the Six Articles encouraged idolatry. All were found guilty of heresy by a rigged jury and burned at the stake.

Simon Alleyn decided, there and then, the fire being too hot for his tender temperament, that he would always follow whatever ordinance was in force.

One day, a man upbraided him in the street, 'Sir, as a clergyman thou art without principle. Thou turneth with the wind.'

He replied, with a wink, 'Not so, for I have always kept my principle: whatsoever king may reign, I shall live and die the Vicar of Bray, sir. Thou canst not turn the wind, yet thou canst turn thy mill to the wind, and so, whatever way the wind shall blow, thy grist shall ever be grinded.'

Dining with the Vicar of Bray

Here is another tale, told of a later, less admirable, perhaps less principled, Vicar of Bray.

The man who stomped into the inn yard was rather plump and looked ungainly, even when standing still. He was slovenly in his dress. He looked – and smelled – like he rarely washed. His eyes were large and protuberant, forever rolling after anyone who came into his presence, like the stable lads who stood gazing at him. He looked confused and lost, as indeed he was – which he tried explaining to them in guttural Scots. He had strayed from his hunting party and found himself alone, until he stumbled upon the Bear Inn.

Uncomprehending, the stable lads just went on staring at this stranger, with his ruddy complexion, his skin slightly pitted by

smallpox, his sparse sandy-coloured hair, and a thin trowel-shaped beard on his long, narrow chin.

The innkeeper came into the yard to see what was to do. The man called out to him, 'What do ye have for ma dinner?'

The innkeeper replied, 'Nothing sir! It be Lent, and all the fish be bespoke and is being dressed for the Vicar of Bray and his Curate.'

The man commanded the innkeeper in a loud voice, 'Well, ma guid man, go ye up to 'em, and say there be a gentleman here who'd be much obliged if they'd allow him to ha' dinner wi' 'em.'

Reluctantly, rather than have a scene, the innkeeper went in and grovellingly asked the Vicar of Bray if a gentleman might dine with them. The Vicar sourly consented to share his dinner with the stranger rather than appear unfaithful to his calling. But he soon regretted any vestige of Christian charity he might have felt; he disliked the man on sight and came to dislike his demeanour even more.

The man's narrow jaws and large tongue made it difficult for him to eat or drink without noisy and disgusting slurping and splashing. The man spoke without ceasing in a barely comprehensible Scots accent and with a very loud voice. The man's mouth was never shut and the soggy, partly masticated repast sprayed across the dining table and place settings.

The man expressed his opinions in stentorian tones with tiresome, infuriating dogmatism. He was constantly nervous, excitable and restless, from time to time springing from his chair and walking up and down on his weak legs with a strangely erratic gait. Worst of all was an aura redolent of the dung heap, which intensified in the warmth of the dining room.

The man's conversation was as ripe as his aroma. He showed an obsessive interest in freaks and monstrosities of nature and in sexual perversions. He said how he loved to listen to obscene stories and to recount them, which he proceeded to do at exhaustive and thankfully incomprehensible length.

The Vicar of Bray made no effort to hide his contempt for the man and his abhorrence of his manners and discourse. The Curate, on the other hand, remained affable throughout the meal. He responded warmly to all the man's opinions, however extreme, 'How true, how true.' He clapped and giggled at all the man's risqué stories, 'What a hoot, what a hoot!' All the while, the Curate replenished the man's plate with poached salmon, filled his glass with spiced wine, plied him with sack and syllabub for dessert, and was altogether an agreeable and attentive host.

If the Vicar despised the man, he despised his Curate's obsequious civilities towards him even more. Moreover, he was puzzled by the Curate's untypical attentiveness towards the man; normally he was a straight-laced, easily distracted, otherworldly sort of clergyman.

When the reckoning arrived, the man delivered the Vicar a further insult, 'Gentlemen, I left ma hame i' haste and forgot ma money. Here I am wi'out a shilling to ma name.'

'A pretty rogue indeed,' quoth the Vicar, glowering at the man with distaste, 'to come and get a meal from us in this way! No, no! You must settle it with the innkeeper. I shall not pay for your dinner, I promise you.'

At this, the Curate piped up, 'Oh! Sir, sir, do not speak thus to the gentleman. I shall pay his share, and think myself well repaid for his good company and amusing conversation, ha ha ha.' The Vicar looked at his Curate, his eyes open wide with amazement at such sycophantic flattery.

Scarcely were these words uttered, when there arose a hubbub in the inn yard, the blowing of horns, the baying of hounds, and a great shout, 'Has anyone seen anything of His Majesty? Has he passed this way?'

The man promptly plumped out his chest, flung wide the balcony doors and stepped out with a flourish. Below him 100 men doffed caps and bent their knees to King James I, as did the astute Curate.

The poor Vicar then bent his knee, mumbling, 'Beg pardon, Majesty, I did not realise …'

'Och, mon! I forgive ye,' His Majesty replied with a roguish glint in his eye, 'Ye'll still be the Vicar of Bray, sir.' Then, turning to the Curate, he said, 'There's a Canonry of Windsor vacant, mon, and it shall be your'n, for we need clerics who can show such obeisance to their sovereign.'

❧

Relaxing after our luncheon, the question arose of how the town came by such a curious name. Professor Gaunt produced an old and battered reprint of Leland's *Itinerary*, edited by Thomas Hearne in 1744, and we were informed that this place had changed its name to Maidenhead in consequence of the exhibition of some holy virgin's head. A local resident, overhearing our conversation, told us that there was a window commemorating this in the new church, but that it was all a nonsense because the name was derived from Maydenehythe, which had something to do with the old timber wharf. He recommended we go down to the river to view the railway viaduct, designed by the late Sir Isambard Kingdom Brunel, which consists of two flat elliptical arches. It is said to have the greatest span of any brick-built bridge in the world and has some remarkable acoustic peculiarities. Had we more time I'm sure we would have enjoyed the walk but, pressed for time as we were, we clambered onto the wagonette and made our way towards Bray.

The church of St Michael was well worth a brief stop; its square tower and plain architecture nestle behind the houses, and even its lychgate is built into a house. The church hasn't always been in the village centre; in the fourteenth century it was a dilapidated building at Builderswell and the villagers had to walk some way on Sundays. The Queen, riding out from Windsor, complained about the state of the church to the Bishop of Salisbury, who ordered that the old church be demolished and rebuilt on the same site. Each day the new walls rose and each night the builders' work was demolished by 'demons'. Church officials decided to move the church into the village of Bray and the new church arose unhindered. Old carvings from the original church were incorporated into the new one, including a Sheela-na-gig, which Henry Rowland was searching for. I offered to help but he seemed unable to give me a reasonable description of what I should be looking for, so I gave up and instead examined the numerous ancient brasses.

Walking round from the church we passed the Hind's Head, no doubt a regular stop for parishioners after Sunday Service, and admired Jesus Hospital, a splendid quadrangle of forty almshouses founded by William Goddard Esq. in 1627:

> Wherein he hath provided for the poore people for ever and lefte it to the sole care and government of the righte worshipful company of Fishmongers of the City of London, of which company he was a free brother.

Sources

Fuller, Thomas, *The Worthies of England*, 1662

Hibbert, Christopher, *The Court at Windsor: A Domestic History*, 1964

Kerry, Charles, *History and Antiquities of the Hundred of Bray*, 1861

Kirkwood, Jean, 'The Windsor Martyrs – Burnt at the Stake', *Windlesora*, No. 27, 2011

Marsh, W.H., *Illustrated Guide to Maidenhead and the Surrounding Country*, 1896

The story of King James I dining with the Vicar of Bray at the Bear Inn in Maidenhead follows the well-documented folk tale. The description of King James' person and manners is taken from the entertaining account in Christopher Hibbert's book.

FIVE

HAWTHORN HILL

Back on the wagonette, and singing lustily about Bray's famous vicar, we rode out of Bray and on towards our next stop, Hawthorn Hill, where Mr Vanderpump told us a story of dreams and treasure.

THE TREASURE OF HAWTHORN HILL

One of the joys of spring in Berkshire is the heavy pinkish-white May blossom on the hawthorn trees, and none are finer than the ancient hawthorn tree which gives its name to Hawthorn Hill.

An innkeeper who kept a small alehouse, the Honey Pot, close to Hawthorn Hill, had a dream. In his dream, he met a man upon the road who said to him, 'If you travel to London Bridge, you will gain riches beyond your wildest dreams.' It seemed a pretty wild dream when he awoke, but the dream nagged at him. Part of him said, 'It's not true, it's just a dream.' Another part replied, 'Yes, but if you don't go to London Bridge you'll wonder for the rest of your life if you've missed out on a fortune.'

In the end he decided to afford himself a short visit to London, where he had never been; if he just happened to cross over London Bridge, well, then he'd find out the truth. Maybe!

London Bridge was a glorious clash of colours and cacophony of sounds. Throngs of people swarmed through the shops and around the stalls, where costers called their wares and small boys tried to filch apples. The innkeeper felt thrilled by all the sights and sounds, and his senses were so overwhelmed that there were times when he had to shut his eyes. 'Well,' he told himself, 'if I find no other treasure, I shall treasure the memory of London Bridge.'

As the innkeeper gazed around, entranced, a stallholder accosted him, 'You look like you want somefink, sir, what can I help you find?'

'Oh,' replied the innkeeper with surprise, 'I'm looking for a fortune. I dreamt I'd find one if I came to London Bridge.'

'There be no fortunes to be found 'ere, 'owever 'ard you work,' said the stallholder, feeling a mite miffed at this waste of his time. 'Mind you, last night I dreamt I'd find a fortune if I went to a 'awthorn 'ill, or some such place, and dug under a tree, but I'm not such a fool as you as to go lookin' for it.' He walked away.

Returning home on the fastest coach, the innkeeper went to Hawthorn Hill and dug under the hawthorn tree, just as the stallholder had said. Beneath the tree, the innkeeper found a crock of gold, full to the brim. He didn't know it, but it was an old Roman pot, and around the rim was a Latin inscription he couldn't read. The stallholder had been spot on. He was also spot on about the innkeeper being a fool, for the profligate and his gold were soon parted. When the gold was gone he left the old pot on a shelf in his inn.

One day, two Oxford scholars called at the inn for refreshment and spotted the empty pot on the shelf, recognising it as Roman. Lifting the pot from the shelf they found the Latin inscription around the rim. They translated the inscription for the innkeeper:

> Beneath the place where this pot stood,
> There is another twice as good.

Once the scholars had departed, the innkeeper returned to the hawthorn tree and dug more deeply. There he found a second crock of gold, full to the brim, twice as big as the first. He didn't know it, but it was a Bronze Age Beaker pot. This time, he used his gold more wisely, and renamed his inn the Money Pot.

SOURCE

Westwood, Jennifer and Simpson, Jacqueline, *The Lore of the Land*, 2006

SIX

WINDSOR

Retracing our route a little, and discussing whether this Berkshire story was older than the Norfolk version that Professor Gaunt was familiar with, we turned onto Drift Road. Our horses gathered speed on this old drovers' road, running straight as an arrow between fields. When we reached New Lodge, near Braywoodside, we asked Mr Beauchamp if he hadn't a story for us. 'Not here,' he replied with a smile.

The road then began to twist and turn between the trees till we met one of the straight roads that runs through Windsor Forest into the heart of the town, where we had booked accommodation for the night at the Royal Oak, a hotel not far from the station.

Windlesora, as the Saxons named this place, means winding shore: Old Windsor is cupped in a curve of the Thames. When William the Conqueror reconstructed the castle above the river, the town relocated itself around the new fortifications. The castle has been occupied and added to by various monarchs ever since, and has kept its importance as a royal seat throughout the centuries.

During the Civil War, there was a Parliamentary garrison at Windsor Castle and the town was Puritan, the resulting rift between royal castle and town taking many years to heal.

The Town Hall, built by Wren in 1686, contains a fine collection of portraits. A bridge across the Thames, built in 1823, connects the borough with Eton. The parish church, dedicated to St John the Baptist, stands in the High Street. It is a plain building in the modern Gothic style, its handsome interior housing many ancient and interesting tombs and monuments, as well as some fine carved oak, the work of Grinling Gibbons.

Having explored the town, and done justice to an excellent dinner, we settled down to hear Mrs Trump's tale of witchcraft. She claimed it had been passed down in her family from one of the witches themselves. It was a far cry from Shakespeare's *Merry Wives*.

THE WITCHES OF WINDSOR

My name's Elizabeth Style, and this is my tale. Though, I confess, not the tale I told the gaoler at Reading before the trial. The tale's not only about me and my sister wise women. It's also about three poor demented souls: Master Richard Galis and his sons Richard and James.

I'm sitting in a dank prison cell in Abingdon, with my friend Margaret and two other old women whom I've always known as Mother Deuell and Mother Dutton. We've been condemned to be hanged as notorious witches. Strangely, as wise women, we have no truck with witchcraft – it is our superstitious, frightened detractors who believe we employ such powers.

My dear old friend Audrey Seidre would have been here with us, if Master Richard Galis hadn't had this frail old woman manhandled into church in front of the congregation. She died, God rest her soul.

Audrey and I grew up together. We watched and learned from our mothers as they worked. They were healers and midwives. They were wise in the lore of the land, the frailties of human bodies, and the mysteries of childbirth. We were destined to follow in their footsteps.

The wisdom our mothers gave us has been known to our female forebears for numberless generations, a wisdom rooted in the time of the old religion, when every plant was seen to possess an enlivening spirit. For, how else would plants know to reach out to the sun, or trees know when to bud?

Our forebears unearthed the secret quality of every plant to heal body and soul. We've inherited this wisdom. Alas, in more recent times, the uprooting and supplanting of the old religion has put women like us in peril. When folk need help in sickness, they turn to us. When they're taught to see us as part of the old religion, they demonise us and accuse us of witchcraft.

Our herbs often have animal-like names: toad flax for problems passing water, cat's ears for jaundice, yellow rattle for women's problems. We give our patients the names of the herbs we use. It's reassuring when we show how familiar we are with their use. If only we'd known how our words would be made to turn and bite us! Our accusers claimed we had 'familiars' – devils in the form of toads, cats and rats, to help us carry out our evil deeds.

As midwives, we're admitted into the mysteries of women's bodies – matters men are ignorant of, arousing in them fear and envy, suspicion and distrust. Besides, childbirth has many hazards which threaten death to mothers and babies. Aye, we can share a mother's joy at the nativity of a healthy child, but when it goes wrong we can suffer rancour, rage and blame.

Our work's mostly been for the poor folk of Windsor. We're paid what little they can afford for healing their diseases and bringing their children into this world. After all that, we end up living in hovels and almshouses, and finally being hounded to our deaths.

Our troubles began some years ago. Mother Dutton was summoned by a distraught Master Richard Galis, thrice Mayor of Windsor, saying that his sons, Richard and James, were possessed by devils. Mother Dutton has a rare gift of seeing deeply into the soul. In Richard and James she saw immense suffering and heartache as well as brimming rage. She treated them both, as she told Master Galis, with a strong dose of chase-devil.[5]

James failed to respond to the treatment. Instead, his rage boiled over, pouring out as obscene curses on Mother Dutton; he threw stones at her house and shouted accusations of witchcraft, calling her 'mother' and 'witch'. Then, he became totally still, his body frozen into a rigid pose, his hand twisted back upon itself. He went completely mad, crying unceasingly, 'Away with the witch!' and had to be confined.

Young Richard claimed he'd been visited by the apparition of a huge and mighty black cat, which crept towards him from the shadows of midnight, filling him with fear and dread. Nevertheless, he seemed to respond well to treatment, and was better able to cope with his afflictions. Yet, he too focused his rage on Mother Dutton and became hell-bent on her destruction; indeed, the destruction of us all.

Master Galis sought vengeance on Mother Dutton for James' madness. He said she had promised to use chase-devil to chase the devils out, but instead had invited more in. He dragged her before the Mayor, Richard Redforth, on a charge of witchcraft. Knowing Master Galis' temperament, Master Redforth ordered Mother Dutton released forthwith.

Galis stormed off, lamenting 'the lack of better magistrates to weed out such malefactors'. Undaunted, shortly afterwards he seized Mother Dutton as she made her way to Clewer, where she

chaſe devill

lived in a straw house, and dragged her to Windsor Gaol. The gaoler, with a knowing shake of his head, refused to take her in without a warrant from the Mayor.

Unrelenting, Master Galis then abducted Mother Dutton, Mother Deuell, Audrey and me, and delivered us to the country house of his friend Robert Handley, who had lost the use of his legs and believed himself bewitched.

Galis demanded that we cure Handley's bewitchment on the threat of being cudgelled. Matters then became confused. Handley insisted we recite the Lord's Prayer and quizzed us on the Ten Commandments. The outcome was that a half-crazed Galis was taken into custody, manacled, and imprisoned – so the gaoler told us – in a deep dungeon that he was lowered into on a rope. He was held without bail, and charged with abduction and false imprisonment.

Alone in his dark cell, deprived of human company, or even a bed, he began to fear he would die there, but after two days the Mayor relented and released him. Of course, he alleged we had used our familiars to incense the Mayor against him and effect his imprisonment. When he later died, his raging son Richard accused us of bringing about his death, calling us 'hellhounds and imps of the devil'.

Richard then became our main detractor, though he often had bouts of lunacy, seeing black cats and fiends with fiery eyes. Once, he tried to burn down Mother Dutton's straw house, by thrusting a cloth dipped in brimstone into it and lighting it with a brand, but the straw was too wet.

The next few years were quiet, on the whole. There were mutterings against us when two butchers, Switcher and Mastlin, died of the plague on their return from London. There was trouble when an ostler refused to pay me, after his wife had a stillbirth, and again after Mother Deuell had spirited away a neighbour's monstrous birth. Richard Galis made various attempts to raise funds after his father died, but his temperament made him unfit for trade and his efforts turned sour. Then, he bought some cattle and sheep, but they were poor stock that mostly died. Of course, in his poor, tormented mind, he saw us despoiling his purse and stock by witchcraft.

During this time, we met Father Rosimond of Farnham Royal. His real name was Osborne, but he decided to change it and set himself up as a Cunning Man after his wife died. She was a wise woman of great skill, and her daughter has followed in her footsteps – a highly intelligent and perceptive young woman. She's well-versed in herbal lore, which she wisely kept hidden from her father. We've tried to keep her name out of all this, so she can continue her good work in peace.

Rosimond asked us to meet him at the marl pit behind Master Dodge's property, but all he wanted was to learn a few tricks from us. We refused, and I reckon he bore a grudge.

Meanwhile, Queen Elizabeth's fear about Catholic plots against her had intensified since her excommunication by Pope Pius V. Like most people in these times, she's deeply superstitious. She's terrified of being killed by witchcraft. So, matters became much worse for us when three wax images with thorns piercing their hearts were found in a London dung heap, representing, it was thought, the Queen and two privy councillors. This was seen as treason.

Richard Galis now had his chance. He searched our homes, and, claiming to have found wax images hidden there, accused us of treason and witchcraft. Wax images, indeed! They were just corn maidens. Women in our families have always made corn maidens from the last sheaf of corn, to hold the spirit of the corn goddess before ploughing her back into the earth to ensure a good harvest the next year.

Galis seized me, tied a rope around me, and dragged me through the streets of Windsor to the castle, to the jeers of the townsfolk. He arrested Margaret and Mother Deuell, but when he went for Mother Dutton she locked herself in a chest and mocked him from inside. However much he fumed, he couldn't get her out, while the fickle crowd ridiculed him. It would've been funny if it hadn't been tragic.

After this affront, Galis had a fit and stormed off to Father Rosimond's home. 'I'm tormented,' he said, 'by infinite pains in body, and by purse ache.' He dragged Rosimond out by his hair, wielding a cudgel, and furiously demanded that the man cure his ailment. Rosimond cried out, 'You are bewitched!' and identified me, Mother Dutton, and Mother Deuell, as the cause.

Well, the privy council appointed the Dean of Windsor, Sir Henry Neville, to find out if we had plotted to kill the Queen by witchcraft. Faced with this impossible task, all he could do was examine us on our religious education, which was precious little, and make us sit beneath the pulpit, in front of all the people, during the service. Then, he sent us to Reading for trial. I was still a strong woman, and walked all the way without discomfort, but after the treatment I received at Reading Gaol I could barely stand.

As we four old wise women sat together in Reading Gaol, we knew there was no hope of justice for us. Everybody, from the Queen downwards, was in an implacable grip of fear and a frenzy of superstition. They needed scapegoats. So, here we were, weak, frail old women, fearing further torture to force confession.

Yet, we felt a quickening strength and power in us – the only power left to us, the power to heal. We chose to confess to the most heinous and villainous enchantments and witchcraft. Yes, partly it was to end the torture, but mainly we had a deeper intention. By holding up to Richard this mirror of his false mental attitude, he might come face to face with himself – and face the truth of his own calumny, and find healing for his soul.

I opted to be the one to make a 'confession' to the gaoler, on behalf of us all, in the presence of Richard Galis, while the other three giggled and sniggered like mad old women: conspiring to murder Master Galis and the butchers Switcher and Mastlin by enchantment and the use of familiars; conspiring to cause James and Richard Galis to be possessed by devils; conspiring to despoil by witchcraft Richard Galis' herds and to cause him purse ache.

The trial was quickly over, and we were brought to Abingdon by cart with a deeply pensive Galis riding alongside. As we trundled along, we sang:

Alas, my love, ye do me wrong
To cast me off discourteously:
And I have lovèd you so long,
Delighting in your company.
I have been ready at your hand,
To grant whatever you would crave.
I have both wagered life and land,
Your love and good will for to have.[6]

As we sang, our words slowly penetrated Richard's mind and pierced his heart. His rage left him. His eyes cleared. For the first time, he saw the whole picture; the injustice that his mad rage had inflicted. Upon his face we saw understanding dawn, chagrin rise, remorse and sorrow surface. But, however much he now desired it, he could not prevent the relentless wheels of Justice from trundling towards the gallows.

Now, our work is done. We shall have a song of thanksgiving on our lips and in our hearts all the way to the scaffold, the threshold of our life beyond.

Sources

Alde, John, pamphlet from 1579

Kupfermann, Elias, 'A Case of Witchcraft in Elizabethan Windsor' in
      Windlesora, No. 27, 2011

Matthews, Tony, *The Witches of Windsor: A Community Play*, 2011

White, Edward, pamphlet from 1579

~

This tale mostly follows John Alde's pamphlet, probably taken
from Richard Galis' extraordinarily candid account. It is told here
from the perspective of the accused women.

The bare bones of the story: In Elizabethan Windsor, four
impoverished old women – Elizabeth Style, Mother Margaret,
Mother Deuell and Mother Dutton – are accused of witchcraft.
The discovery of three wax images, with thorns through their
hearts, in a London dung heap, brings their case to national
prominence when similar images are found in the homes of the
accused witches. The three images are thought to represent Queen
Elizabeth and two privy councillors and are therefore treasonable.

In the furore which follows, the four women are arrested and
imprisoned at Reading. Elizabeth Style makes a detailed confession
that she and the three others accused used their 'familiars' – a toad,
cat and rat – to bring about the deaths of prominent Windsor
citizens, and some cattle. After being tried and convicted, they are
hanged at Abingdon on 28 February 1579.

WINDSOR GREAT PARK

The following morning we took a little time for one last look around this historic town. Those of us who felt the need for a little more exercise before resuming our journey joined Mr Vanderpump and Mr Beauchamp for a brisk walk by the river. It was soon time to board the wagonette and head through Windsor Great Park towards Ascot. Soon after we left the tree-dotted open parkland, we came to a roadside inn, the Duke of Edinburgh, at a place called Woodside. Here we stopped for an excellent cup of coffee and my brother told one of Berkshire's most famous legends, 'Herne the Hunter'.

James Easton, the landlord, was most interested in this tale, as one of his ancestors had been employed with the royal buckhounds.

HERNE THE HUNTER AND THE WILD HUNT

Wandering out of Windsor Great Forest onto Bagshot Heath, the boy saw smoke rising from a rude hut of clay-covered wattle and daub which he had not seen before. Here he met Philip Urswick, on the first of many visits.

Philip wore a coarse, black, woollen, belted tunic over black hose, with black leather boots, a black cowl and a black scowl upon his face. 'What took you so long, boy?' Philip uttered, as the boy hesitantly pushed open the hut door, 'Now you're here, come in and take a stool by the fire. We have much to do, and it's time we made a start.'

Nonplussed by this stranger's greeting, the boy did as he was bid. Over the coming months, the pair spent many days crawling and stalking around Windsor Great Forest, or storytelling by the

fire in Philip's small hut. Philip taught the boy all he knew about the craft of questing, tracking and hunting the wild hart.

In their long talks in the flickering firelight, Philip spoke of the monstrous black dog, Bogey Beast, which roamed his home country of Furness. Whenever this creature was seen prowling the graveyards, highways and moors with bared fangs, sharp claws and eyes ablaze, fear, mayhem and death would surely follow – the destroying of harvests, the wrecking of ships, the engulfing of villages. These many griefs afflicted Philip's soul. They darkened his countenance. His endurance of grief had won him a harsh and uncanny wisdom and conjured a devilish enterprise.

Philip told the boy, 'In Furness, the time of the Danelaw seems not so long ago, and by winter firesides folk still tell the old tales of the gods, and of Odin, mightiest of the gods.' He added with a rare chuckle, 'You Anglo-Saxons might know him as Woden.'

Over the months, Philip told the boy all he knew about Woden; how he gave one eye for one sip of the water of insight, thereby gaining immense knowledge and a thirst for wisdom;

how he hanged himself from the great tree of sacrifice, the axis of the world; how, hanging from the windswept tree for nine long nights, he died to win wisdom known only to the dead, and rose from death to bring that wisdom to the world of the living; how he led the Wild Hunt across the night sky, riding his eight-legged horse Sleipnir, flanked by fierce wolves Freki and Geri, with ravens Huginn and Muninn circling his brow, and following behind him all the dead who ever rode to hunt.

Philip drew no distinction between fact and fable, Wild Hunt being as much part of his commonplace world as wild hart. As the boy absorbed Philip's tales by the warmth of the hut fire, Woden entered his soul. The boy adopted the name 'Herne', which Philip told him was one of Woden's many names and meant 'Leader of the Wild Hunt'. The image of himself as Leader of the Wild Hunt filled his young heart with joy. Thus the tale of Herne the Hunter begins.

In dawn's pale light, Herne the Hunter was in Windsor Great Forest with his cunning hound Fríge and his ravenous alaunts Freki and Geri, questing for his quarry – a mighty red deer. Herne carefully followed the deer's lay, its tracks, droppings, broken branches and scent rubbings.

As King Richard came into the forest at sunrise with his nine keepers and his pack of hunting dogs, Herne approached and knelt before him, saying, 'Sire! I have located the lay of a thirty-tine hart and would offer this to you.' The King accepted Herne's offer with glee, to the covert vexation of the nine keepers, and the hunt began.

Relays of hounds were positioned along the lay to ensure the dogs were not worn out before the hart tired. Then came the 'fynding'; Fríge was released to find the hart. When the lymer located the hart, the chase began, with the keepers keeping the hounds on the track of their quarry. When the hart tired and could run no further, it turned, lowering its immense antlers to defend itself from the hunting dogs. But the dogs were ordered to hold back, to allow the King to approach the hart with a long spear to plunge into its heart. The deer was butchered by ancient ritual, for in those times hunters revered their quarry, and the hounds were rewarded with the entrails and sweetbreads as their portion.

''Twere a fine hunt, Herne, and a fine kill,' said the King, and after that Herne was forever at the King's side when he went to hunt. But the other nine keepers envied Herne's woodcraft skills and his favour with the King, and looked for ways to discredit him.

In the forest at that time was an old forty-tine stag who by its cunning and strength had always evaded the hunt. Now, by the combined skill of Herne, his lymer Fríge, and his alaunts Freki and Geri, the old stag was at bay in a small clearing, his menacing forty-tined antlers lowered in defence. The King was moving forward for the kill with his long spear, when the hart made a swift lunge and with a turn of its antlers gored the King's horse, throwing him from the saddle. Just as the hart moved to despatch the defenceless king, Herne flung himself in its path and was grievously pierced in his side. In his last moments before darkness descended, Herne stabbed the hart in the throat and its life bled out.

There and then, the King gathered the hunting party together, swore an oath that if Herne lived he would make him head keeper, and promised ten gold nobles to anyone who could save Herne's life.

'I can bring him back to life,' said a voice, and all eyes turned towards a man dressed all in black, riding a black stallion.

The King was affronted. 'What are you doing in my forest? You must be a poacher.'

The nine keepers readily agreed that the man was a poacher, muttering that Herne should just be put out of his misery.

'I am Philip Urswick. I live on Bagshot Heath, where I joined the hunt this day,' said the man in black, 'and I can bring this man back to life and restore him to you in a month.'

While the nine keepers were swearing loudly that they had not seen Philip join the hunt, the King interjected, 'If you really can cure this man, I shall give you the reward and a free pardon for your offences against the Crown; otherwise I will see you hanged.'

With a nod to the King and a wry smile, and to the astonishment of the King and keepers, Philip deftly cut the antlers off the deer with his hunting knife and tied them onto Herne's head. Then he ordered a stretcher to be made of poles and branches, and instructed that Herne be carried to his hut by four of the keepers, with the other five following behind.

Upon arriving at Bagshot Heath, the keepers were still muttering curses against Herne. To advance his dark and devious designs, Philip made a bargain with the keepers. He agreed to bring Herne back to life shorn of his woodcraft and hunting skills, and in return the nine keepers, having no wealth to offer, agreed to do the first thing that Philip would command of them.

After a month, though still in pain from his pierced side, Herne returned to Windsor Castle. The King presented him with 100 silver groats, a silver hunting horn, and lodgings in the castle for saving his life. However, when the King realised that Herne had lost all his hunting skills, rather than appointing him as head keeper, he discharged him from his service.

Herne was outraged by the King's callous dismissal and betrayal. He rode off into Home Park, found an ancient oak tree, and hanged himself from it. Like his exemplar Woden, he had been pierced in the side, and like Woden, he hung from the windswept tree for nine long nights. A passing pedlar finally saw Herne's corpse hanging from the tree, but by the time he had fetched the keepers the body was gone.

That night, Herne's Oak, as folk called it thereafter, was blasted by lightning; like Woden's tree – whose roots were gnawed by dragons, whose leaves were nibbled by deer, whose flesh was torn by goats – Herne's tree became a suffering tree.

Philip's cunning cantrip, which had robbed Herne of his hunting skills, also robbed the nine keepers of theirs. Rather than risk the King's displeasure, and put their livelihoods and even their lives at peril, they consulted Philip. He told them the only way to rid themselves of the curse and restore their hunting skills was to come to Herne's Oak at midnight.

When the nine keepers arrived at Herne's Oak, to their dismay Herne appeared before them transformed. His mighty forty-tine antlers were no longer tied to his head, but grew from his skull. He ordered them to return at midnight the next night with horses and hounds, ready to hunt. Then he vanished from their sight.

The next night at midnight the nine keepers rode with their hounds to Herne's Oak. Herne awaited them with Freki and Geri. He was mounted upon an eight-legged horse. Two ravens eyed the keepers from their perches in the stricken oak tree.

Herne led the nine keepers deep into the forest, galloping many miles, until they reached a clearing, where Philip Urswick appeared to them. Philip commanded the nine keepers to fulfil their bargain by serving Herne and joining his hunting party. Philip Urswick had reached the culmination of his devious and demonic enterprise.

That night, and for many nights after, Herne's hunting party careered through Windsor Great Forest. Herne was at its head, mounted upon his eight-legged steed, flanked by Freki and Geri. The ravens circled his brow. The nine keepers and all their hounds followed at his heels.

This was no careful hunt, carried out with reverence for the quarry, ending the chase with a clean kill and ritual butchery. This was a wild chase. The herds of deer were scattered and decimated. Stags, hinds and fawns were mercilessly pursued, slaughtered, and torn apart by the voracious and bloodthirsty dogs.

The King was enraged by this ravaging of his herds and the loss of good sport in his own forest. He interrogated his terrified keepers until they confessed that they were in thrall to Herne, and then he demanded they escort him to Herne's Oak at midnight to speak with Herne himself.

'Why are you destroying my herds of deer?' asked the King.

'For vengeance,' replied Herne, 'against those nine keepers who sought my downfall.'

Then Herne made a bargain with the King; he would not call out the Wild Hunt during the King's reign, provided the King hanged the nine keepers from the same tree on which he had hanged himself. Then Herne vanished from the King's sight.

The King kept his side of the bargain. The next day he had the nine keepers hanged from Herne's Oak. Herne also kept his promise. He did not call out the Wild Hunt during the King's reign. Soon after the King's death, the Wild Hunt was seen again, tearing apart the night sky, rampaging through Windsor Great Forest, leaving chaos and carnage in its wake.

Among the Wild Hunt were the nine keepers, their faces gaunt and grim, with all their savage hounds. At its head, Herne had taken his wished-for place as Leader of the Wild Hunt, riding his eight-legged horse, flanked by fierce alaunts Freki and Geri, with ravens circling his brow, and following behind him all the dead who ever rode to hunt.

Beware the Wild Hunt! Like the Bogey Beast, whenever the Wild Hunt is seen, careering across the night sky with Herne the Hunter at its head, fear, mayhem and death shall surely follow.

Sources

Fitch, Eric, *In Search of Herne the Hunter*, 1994
Crossley-Holland, Kevin, *The Norse Myths*, 1980

The traditional folk tale of Herne the Hunter is unique to Windsor Great Forest, though stories of the Wild Hunt exist throughout Europe.

The earliest reference to Herne the Hunter is in Shakespeare's *The Merry Wives of Windsor*, though it seems likely he knew of a pre-existing local oral tradition.

The story of Herne the Hunter, as told here, follows the traditional folk tale recounted by Eric Fitch, except in the following respects:

1. The character and role of the enigmatic Philip Urswick – including the early part of the story, prior to Herne's meeting with King Richard II – is inferred from the sparse particulars about Philip given in the traditional folk tale.
2. The subtle connection and parallel between the tale of Herne the Hunter and that of Odin/Woden is made more clear-cut.

EIGHT

BRACKNELL

With the ghostly cries of the Wild Hunt still ringing in our ears, we continued through the woods to the edge of Royal Ascot, where Mr Beauchamp pointed out the road that leads to the royal kennels, where Her Majesty's buckhounds are kept. Looking across to the other side of the road, Mr Vanderpump informed us that construction of the racecourse beyond the trees had been at the prompting of the Duke of Cumberland in the reign of George III. If our journey had been a month earlier, these roads would have been thronged with royal, noble and fashionable crowds. Dr Benjamin then drew our attention to the London and Ascot Hospital for Convalescents and Incurables, an extensive institution built just forty years ago. At the crossroads we turned east towards the village of Bracknell, having decided against a detour to explore Tower Hill and Bagshot Heath, where Claude Du Vall danced his famous courante.

When we reached Bracknell, Mr Cleave pointed out the notorious inn named the Hind's Head, whose landlord is said to have been as duplicitous as the one who ended Thomas Cole's life. The trapdoor here was by the bed, and dropped unwary travellers into a well. Unfortunately for the landlord, the serving girl took a fancy to one young farmer destined for this fate, and, having warned him of the trap, helped him drop a weighted bundle down the shaft. She then escaped with him out the window. The young man returned with a group of labourers from a nearby farm, and the murderous innkeeper and his friends were dragged off to justice.[7]

From Bracknell we took the Crowthorne road that runs between South Hill Park and Easthampstead Park, the latter being a favourite royal hunting lodge. When we reached Nine Mile Ride, which runs parallel to the old Roman road that the locals call Devil's Highway, we turned east and stopped at Caesar's Camp, where Mr Beauchamp told another tale about King James.

KING JAMES AND THE TINKER

It was with mixed feelings, on that cold April day, that James began his progress from his Scottish kingdom to receive the crown and sceptre of England. At the age of thirty-six, he was loath to forsake his beloved Scotland for an alien land, yet he had long relished the prospect of seizing without force the land of his country's historic southern neighbour and adversary.

Now, he was not only King James VI of Scotland but also King James I of England. Well, he would survive the English court. He had survived much worse: an austere upbringing with frequent beatings; the absence of loving parents or any affection at all; a rigorous religious instruction in the Protestant faith as an instrument of State policy; surrounded always by hard, dour, dogmatic, and ambitious men who saw him only as a means to advance their own power and influence.

The prospect of being King of England was quite agreeable, but the reality! Well, his basket of bright ideas had been received like a bucket of bad oysters. Take his idea of being called 'King of Great Britain' – and Ireland and France of course, it goes without saying – after all, he was already King of England and King of Scotland; as he said, 'Hath He not made us all in one island, compassed with one sea and of itself by nature indivisible?'

The Commons resisted – threw it out, actually. Even his own Scottish Parliament threw it out. Well, he showed them; he had himself declared 'King of Great Britain' by proclamation. Hmm! Then, that pompous, boorish, braggart Bacon told him to his face that he could not legally use the title.[8]

Anyway, it's only politics. Then again, trying to blow him up in his own Parliament is too much politics. Blow up Parliament, fine, but not with him in it!

What really made him gag on his oat cakes was the English court. He was accustomed to rough Scottish barons who spoke their minds, 'My aye shall be aye an' my nay shall be nay, as we say in Scotland,' but these English courtiers were nought but fawning, effete buffoons with their rag-wristed curtseys and curdled wits. Ugh! Yet, where the Scots were simple and direct, these English were sly and scheming, all soft words and insinuations, like cats wheedling to win the cream of the kingdom.

To escape from the pinpricks of politics, James liked to stay at his hunting lodge in Easthampstead Park – which he had developed for the princely sum of £250 – and hunt the deer in Windsor Great Forest. Alas, he oftentimes found himself trailed by manipulative and officious courtiers with their sibilant speech, 'We'll seek a stag for you, Sire. The servants have one saved for you, Sire. Simply stay, Sire, and a fine stag will soon streak from yonder thicket, Sire, an easy slay for you, Sire.'

One day, with rising fury and revulsion, and to the courtiers' consternation, James simply spurred his tall, black stallion and galloped away. He cantered through the forest for a while until he reached the side of the wood, coming out in Blackbird Lane, where he found an inn, the Royal Black Bridge.

Entering the inn, James saw an old tinker nursing a jug of ale with one hand and circling it with his other arm.

'Honest fellow,' James addressed the tinker in his tight wee Scots tongue, 'What hast thee in thy jug that thou hugst say tight?'

'Is it not a jug of the nappy brown ale?' replied the tinker in his soft Irish brogue, with a sibilance so much more appealing than that of those accursed courtiers.

'Nappy brown ale is it? Yon's a fine Scots word, "nappy", I've nay heard this many a while.'

'Aye, a fine word to be sure, and a fine jug of it, and I hug it to mysel' for I come of a large family and had to learn to protect my own, did I not?'

'Truly, sir, we must take care to protect our own,' said James, 'And now sir, I trust you will allow for me to purchase a pitcher of this nappy brown ale for the each of us?'

'I wish you good health for it,' quoth the tinker. 'And though thy attire is most gallant and fine, in truth ye shall find, when we have drained these pitchers, my two pence be as good as thine. For, I am my own man, beholden to no other of whatever degree.'

'Nay, by my soul, thou speaketh true, and no man shall gainsay thee.'

So, they supped awhile in quiet companionship before James spoke again.

'Pray tell me, good sir, what news is around this day? For I have heard nought.'

'Why, sir, I hear the King do ride in Windsor Forest, entertaining the deer.'

'Ha! Ha! Entertainment is it? More like they enter torment.'

So, the King and the tinker enjoyed the friendly camaraderie of strangers in an alien land. For the King it was refreshing finally to encounter an agreeable companion in England who was his own man, willing to speak his own mind. At last, the tinker expressed a hope one day to see the King.

'To be sure, long is the time I have travelled these lands, but in all my days I have never known the happiness of seeing the King himself, as I would wish to do, whilst he be a-hunting the deer.'

With a brisk laugh, the King replied, 'If thou canst ride as well as though doest converse, thou canst get up behind me and I shall bring thee into the royal presence of King James himself.'

'By the Holy Saints, that would be a happy thing for me altogether, there be no doubt about that. Though, perchance, all the lords will be dressed so fine I shall hardly know His Majesty from the rest.'

Never in all his sojourns in this alien country had James laughed so heartily.

'By my truth, there be a way to discover the King, for all the rest will be bare-headed, only the King's head will be covered.'

With that, James mounted his black stallion. The tinker mounted behind, clutching a stout leather bag with his precious tools: his big shears, hand snips and nippers, stakes and fire pot, soldering iron and hunk of solder. Thus laden, the black stallion bore them into the forest to meet the bewildered courtiers, still scouring the forest for the King.

As the King entered their presence, they immediately doffed their caps and set about waggling their wrists, bowing and curtseying, and loudly declaring their efforts in searching for their liege lost in the Great Forest.

James and the tinker dismounted and looked around at the antics of the courtiers.

The tinker spoke softly into the King's ear, 'Since all are arrayed in such gallant finery, pray, tell me sir, which one is the King?'

Loudly quoth the King in a grave and perplexed tone, 'By my soul, man, you or I must be the King, for see around ye, all the rest are bare-headed.'

The tinker placed his bag of tools carefully upon the ground, and then followed it by falling upon his knees. Acting as if frightened clear out of his wits, the tinker began to bawl. 'Mercy, Majesty, for my manifold offences against the dignity of thy royal person.' Then quietly, he said, 'Yet, Sire, it hath been a braw afternoon with fine company.'

'Be not afraid, thou art a good and agreeable fellow,' said James, a wide grin, unfamiliar to his flabbergasted court, cracking his dour cheeks. 'Tell me your name.'

'Why, Sire, my name's John o' the Vale, mender of kettles and lover of nappy brown ale.'

Unsheathing his sword, James laid it gently upon the tinker's shoulder, 'Arise, then, Sir John o' the Vale, Mender of the King's Kettles, Knight of 500 crowns a year. From this time on, the King shall have an agreeable companion who loves nappy brown ale and speaks his mind, and my beloved Queen Anne shall possess the finest kettles in the whole of Christendom.'

SOURCES

Child, Francis James, *The English and Scottish Popular Ballads*, Volume 5, 2003

Vincent, James Edmund, *Highways and Byways of Britain: Berkshire Forest District*, 1906

꙳

The bare bones of the story: Whilst hunting in Windsor Great Forest, King James leaves his nobles and goes to an inn, where he meets and drinks with a tinker. The tinker has never seen the King and wishes to do so. The King says to get up behind him and they'll ride to see His Majesty. The tinker fears he will not know the King from his lords and is told the King will be the only one whose head is covered. When they meet the lords, the tinker asks which is the King. 'Why,' says the King, 'It must be you or I, for the rest are uncovered.' The tinker falls on his knees asking for mercy, but the King takes his sword and makes the tinker a knight with 500 crowns a year.

BRIMPTON

Returning to Nine Mile Ride, we turned west through Wick Hill to the end of the Ride, where we turned left. About a mile down the road, we turned right towards Arborfield. Turning left before reaching the village, we travelled through Farley Hill to Swallowfield for lunch at the George and Dragon.

After our rest, we felt the need for some exercise, so we walked up to All Saints' Church. The Revd Plumb informed us that this church was supposedly erected by John le Despenser, Lord of Beaumys, in the thirteenth century, but parts of the church may be even older. The unusual mix of grey flint walls and brick tower, surrounded by trees, house some beautiful stained-glass windows and interesting monuments.

Back at the road we walked across two bridges over the River Blackwater, and admired the view over Swallowfield Park, before boarding the wagonette for the next stage of our journey. Driving through Swallowfield village, we travelled north towards Spencers Wood before turning left through Mortimer and Aldermaston until we came to Brimpton. There was once a preceptory of the Knights Templar here, but no sign of it remains today. The church, which was built thirty years ago, may cover the site of any buildings from the time of the Knights Templar.

Brimpton is one of the villages said to have had a witch, so it was here, in the snug at the Three Horseshoes, that we met up with four men who, in their travels round the county, had amassed a wealth of local witchcraft tales.

FOLK TALES ABOUT BERKSHIRE WITCHES

Jonas and Dobbin, Shadrach and Angel, with foaming tankards
before them and pipes between their teeth, were swapping yarns.
For starters, they totted up (between pulling on their pints and
drawing on their pipes) how many folk, to their knowledge, had
met the Inglesham ghost, who appears in the shape of a fierce black
dog with slavering jaws and cruel canine teeth. Then Shadrach
piped up, 'Now, the Brimpton Witch, she were a bad 'un, right
spiteful and resentful, and could frighten and even hurt people by
magic.' He then told us the following story.

The Brimpton Witch: Passing Through Glass

A young man, who lived in the neighbouring cottage to the witch,
cut down a currant bush which obstructed the light from his
window. However, the bush was in the witch's garden, and as a
punishment she plagued him unmercifully.

Her favourite trick, whenever she saw him in his garden, was to
raise him off the ground by magic and hurl him at the glass window
of his cottage. Each time, as he hurtled towards the window, he
feared he would be cut to pieces by the broken glass, but she made
him pass through the glass without cutting
himself. In speaking about this
to another villager, he said he
didn't know how it could be
true, because he wasn't cut and
there was no blood on the glass.

Another of her tricks, he told
the other villager, was to knock
on his door, and when he
answered she would turn herself into glass slippers and chase
him round his house. He said
he was scared stiff all the time, even
inside his own cottage, because he knew for
certain she could turn herself into a hare and
pass through a keyhole, as he had seen her do.

Weary of the witch's persecution, the young man consulted the local carrier, who seemed like a person who got about a bit and knew his onions. The local carrier brought the young man a sheep's liver, telling him, 'Nail this up over your mantelshelf, and when the old witch plagues you again, stick a pin into it. Every pin you stick into it, she will feel stuck into her own body.'

The man followed this advice with great success, for he had no more trouble from the witch next door.

Coleshill: Old Betty's Pranks

'Do you remember Old Betty?' chortled Angel, 'My, what pranks she played! She was famed all around Coleshill for her many evil tricks and was a sore trouble to the carters, cowmen, and shepherds round about, bringing the flocks and herds and pregnant mares under her powerful spell and working incalculable mischief upon all and sundry. At one time, the lambs, calves, and foals were still-born. The gates and doors would fall off their hinges. The pumps wouldn't draw water. The cream wouldn't set in the broad pans. The cobbler couldn't work his wax while she was near. Half the people of the countryside fell sick.

'All the while, Old Betty danced in the streets at midnight and spat up hundreds of pins and young crows, as the villagers confidently believed.

'Anyway, she came to a bad end and now lies buried on the roadside, 3 miles away from here.'

Faringdon: The Witch and the Pig

Jonas, the ox-carter, laughed aloud as he remembered a tale he'd heard on his travels. 'There was this witch in Faringdon who had tampered with her neighbour's pig, causing it to go mad in the sty, oinking noisily and flinging itself about.

'The owner of the animal, a farm labourer, was distressed at the occurrence and was uncertain what to do. Then, being a bit gormless, he thought, if you can cure people by bleeding them, then you can cure a pig the same way. Accordingly, he took his shears and snipped a piece out of the pig's ear, causing it to bleed profusely.

'A moment later, behold! Out of her house ran the old witch, holding her ear, with blood gushing between her fingers. It appears that, for a prank, the witch had conjured her spirit to enter the pig. When the swine's ear was cut, the witch's spirit was still inside the pig, so she was injured as well.'

Dobbin, Shadrach and Angel laughed till they choked on their smoke at such a daft story, then they cleared their throats and gobbed into the spittoon.

Jonas waited with a sly grin, anticipating the end of the story, 'Happily, the pig recovered, but the villagers left the old woman alone, and very soon she bled to death.'

Now the men were subdued and sat ruminating a while, till Dobbin was put in mind of another horror story.

Newbury: Witches Buried Alive

'Down the road in one of the villages near Newbury, within the memory of some of the older folk, three witches were 'buried quick', or buried alive as you townsfolk would say. They were buried standing, up to their necks, with just their heads above ground, and were left there to die of thirst and starvation – a terrible death you might say, but the local folk, well, they must have had their reasons.

'They must have still had their tongues, which I reckon got lots of exercise, with plenty of cussing and hexing and blaspheming and fuming going about.

'The story goes that one of the three wretched women lived longer than the other two, because someone threw her an apple core to eat. How could she have eaten the apple, I'd like to know, if her arms were covered by the earth? Happen, as the woman was credited with being a witch, we can only conclude she was also endowed with extraordinary powers.

'I have heard the story, with every detail the same, from many of the old people living in the villages, quite far apart from each other, so something of the kind must have happened.'

Well, by that time the four men had supped enough ale, smoked enough baccy and swapped enough yarns, so they roused themselves to meander home, each thinking to himself, 'I reckon I'll keep well away from witches.'

Sources

Berkshire Local History Committee, Reference Z1-17; recorded by Lady
　　Muriel Percy, November 1937
Berkshire Local History Library
Reading Mercury, 23 September 1961
Salmon, Miss L., *Untravelled Berkshire*, 1909
Williams, Alfred, *Round about the Upper Thames*, 1915; 2010

In these sources, especially in the files of the Berkshire Local History Committee, we hear the authentic voices of Berkshire people recording folk tales as they have been told them.

Coleshill has been called 'The Flower of Berkshire'.

TEN

NEWBURY

From Brimpton we took the country lanes past Greenham Common and entered Newbury from the south. Nyuburi plundered the nearby ruins of the Roman station Spinae for building materials, and the occasional Roman brick can still be spotted in the town. It is mentioned in Saxon records, and a castle was built here by an early owner of the manor.

Mr Beauchamp informed us that King John often visited the town when hunting at Kingsclere, and an ancient ballad tells of his concealment in the house of an old spinning woman here when he fled from his insurgent barons. In gratitude for his escape, he founded the almshouses, now called St Bartholomew's Hospital.

In Tudor times, the town rose to high eminence as a seat of broadcloth manufacture. John Smallwood, better known as 'Jack of Newbury', found fortune and fame in the town. Christopher Shoemaker also found fame, but through ill-fortune. He was one of the Newbury Martyrs, burned at the stake in 1514 for 'reading the Gospels to a listener'. Parliamentarians and Royalists fought two bloody battles nearby. Several mounds covering the remains of the slain can be seen on the Wash battlefield, and relics of the fight are still occasionally found. But it was of an earlier conflict, between King Stephen and the Empress Maude, that we were to hear this evening, at the Black Bear in the Marketplace, where the landlord John Hewett had prepared a sumptuous supper for us. David had arranged a meeting with local historian and author Walter Money, who told us one of the many tales he has collected:

Playing Soldiers with the King

It was a time of anarchy. There was civil war between the usurping King Stephen and his cousin Empress Maude, self-styled Lady of the English, bringing disturbance throughout England, not least in the county of Berkshire. In the void created by the collapse of the King's peace, avaricious local lords made petty wars, raiding and fighting one another, building unauthorised 'adulterine' castles to defend their spoils, and causing serious devastation to the land and its people.

One such was John Marshall. He built an adulterine motte-and-bailey in the parish of Hamstead Marshall, close to the town of Newbury, which was within his fief. The fire of civil war had been reignited by the arrival in England of an army led by Henry FitzEmpress, Empress Maude's warlike eldest son, and it suited John Marshall to align himself with Henry.

King Stephen arrived with his army at Newbury Castle, which protected the road to Wallingford. Before the castle gates, King Stephen summoned the constable to open up and deliver the castle into his hands. When the constable refused, and an assault on the garrison was repulsed, the King embarked on a siege of Newbury castle and town.

After a time, John Marshall asked for a truce, while he gained permission from Henry FitzEmpress – or so he claimed – to surrender the castle, offering his five-year-old son William as hostage. The truce was granted, but John Marshall used this respite to strengthen his garrison and replenish his supplies. When the truce expired he refused to surrender the castle.

Enraged by John's deceit, King Stephen demanded that John Marshall surrender the castle immediately or watch his young son hanged before the castle walls. John replied callously, 'Do as you will. I have the hammer and the anvil to forge still better sons.'

So be it. As the King led William to the place of his execution, the boy chattered all the while, pleased to escape the stifling atmosphere of the siege and to be in the open air. Oblivious of the sombre scaffold to which he was being led, William talked cheerfully to the King about the starlings flocking in the trees, the crows leisurely searching for carrion, the gorse and broom that had encroached on the abandoned fields, anything which caught his eye.

The Earl of Arundel was standing at the place of execution, and, as they approached, William spotted the javelin he held. He asked to look at it and studied it for some time, talking with Arundel about how the pointed steel head was riveted onto a 4ft ash pole and discussing with him the way the javelin could be used in battle. The King was so taken with William's artless enthusiasm and curiosity that he shrank from harming the child and ordered him to be taken back to camp. The execution was postponed.

Sometime later, as the siege became protracted, the King was persuaded by his advisors to have William flung over the castle ramparts from a siege engine, a counterweight trebuchet. As the King led William towards the trebuchet, the child cried out in delight, 'Oh, look, what a beautiful swing, and it's just my size!'

The King was acutely affected by the contrast between the child's innocent delight and his father's callous and careless cupidity. More than this, he saw mirrored in John Marshall's unnatural cruelty his own duplicity in breaking his oath to King Henry I: Stephen had promised to honour the succession of Empress Maude, Henry's daughter and his own cousin, to the throne of England, a throne which he had later usurped.

Chastened, and sensible as he was to the graces of infancy, the King's heart melted. He had the trebuchet's sling lowered a little and, lifting William into it, he gave him a swing. Unwittingly, the child had transformed the apparatus of his death into an instrument of his play.

Then said the King, his voice husky with emotion, 'Take the boy away. One would need a heart of iron to see such a child perish.' The execution was postponed indefinitely.

As the siege dragged on, Stephen spent a good part of his time, the best part, entertaining his young prisoner. They walked and talked through fields overgrown with gorse and broom bushes. William was fascinated by the golden yellow flowers of broom, the wild bees buzzing around and alighting upon them, and the way the flowers exploded, scattering their pollen over the insects.

William told the King he thought the flowers looked like soldiers' helmets. He cut the long stems, which he said looked like tall soldiers, and taught the King a game of 'playing soldiers' with the stems, which he used to play with his mother Sybilla. Playing soldiers with the eager young boy was altogether more gratifying to King Stephen than playing soldiers in reality with his inhumane father.

Throughout the five-month siege, King Stephen was in negotiation with Henry FitzEmpress. Through friendship with young William and contempt for his father's treachery, Stephen had begun to contemplate his own perfidy, and he agreed to declare Henry as heir to the throne. By playing soldiers with the King, young William had prevented an attack on the town and castle of Newbury, saving many lives, and had created space for a negotiated peace.

SOURCE

Money, Walter, *The History of the Ancient Town and Borough of Newbury in the County of Berkshire*, 1887

❦

The probable site of John Marshall's motte-and-bailey castle is near the village of Hamstead Marshall, though only the motte remains.

The Siege of Newbury Castle was in the year 1152. In 1154, King Stephen died and was succeeded by King Henry II, eldest son of Empress Maude, whose throne he had usurped.

William Marshall grew up to be a brave and distinguished knight, and for a while served Henry's queen, Eleanor of Aquitaine.

ELEVEN

SPEEN

The next morning, after a good breakfast, we set out to explore Newbury town, with its broad, well-paved streets and many ancient houses, several of which are interesting for their architecture or historical associations. The Corn Exchange is a handsome and commodious building in the Italian style. A neat stone bridge takes the principal thoroughfare across the Kennet.

The parish church of St Nicholas is a spacious building of stone in the late Perpendicular style, with octagonal turrets on the western tower. Here, we were told by a passing local, Hannah Snell was married on 3 November 1759. This remarkable woman was abandoned by her first husband. Undeterred, she disguised herself as a man and went in search of him. Her disguise was so successful that she was pressed into the English army, and then joined the marines, managing to conceal her sex for four and a half years. It was only when she left the service that she revealed herself to be a woman, becoming the toast of London and appearing on stage, dressed in her uniform and thrilling audiences with tales of her adventures in England, Scotland and India.

The wagonette collected us outside the Literary and Scientific Institution, where Dr Benjamin had been looking round their excellent library and the geological collection in the museum connected to it. The Art and Technical Institute next door had drawn Professor Gaunt.

Travelling west on the Great West Road, we turned north to Speen. Just past the Hare and Hounds Hotel is a crossroads, at which we turned left towards the church. There is a striking obelisk at the junction, which is apparently the first gas lamp to be erected in the district. It was moved here from the Broadway last year to make way for the new Jubilee Clock.

A short way along the road, we came to the green lane that runs down to the church. A little way down this lane on the right is the narrow muddy path to the Ladywell, an ancient sacred spring reputed to have miraculous healing properties for eye diseases and other ills. This spot was the place chosen by Revd Plumb to tell his tale, but the place was so damp, cramped and neglected that we retired to the nearby churchyard to hear it. A passing sexton heard our complaint and said he would pass on to the vicar our suggestion that the place be tidied up, though how long it would take the parish council to act on the suggestion he couldn't say. Finding a suitable corner, we listened to tales of the saintly King Edward the Confessor.

LEGENDS OF EDWARD THE CONFESSOR

King Edward was the last king of the House of Wessex. Later, he

acquired the epithet 'The Confessor' for his unworldliness, his profound piety and his devotion to the Church. So devoted was he, that before his marriage to Edith of Wessex he vowed to remain celibate. All the same, she is portrayed with a secret smile upon her lips, a twinkle in her upturned eyes, and a bloom upon her cheek.

King Edward was a man of such saintliness and humility that he was well-fitted to discharge that God-given faculty of kings: touching ill people to cure them. In fact, it was he who conceived this long-standing royal tradition, which faithful monarchs espoused for another 700 years.

No tale speaks more tellingly of this St Edward the Confessor, as we must call him, than that of the pilgrimage of Wulwin Spillecorn.

Wulwin Spillecorn's Pilgrimage

Long ago, in the time of King Edward the Confessor, there was a wood-cutter by the name of Wulwin Spillecorn, the son of a Saxon yeoman, Wulmar of Nutgareshale. After a hard, tiring morning, felling and cutting timber in Bernwood Forest, weariness came upon Wulwin and he lay down under a shady tree and fell fast asleep. As the sun moved around, it fell full on his face, causing (William of Malmesbury sagely suggests) his eyeballs to fill with blood. When he awoke, he found, to his surprise and consternation, that he had been struck blind.

Wulwin stumbled out of the forest and found his way to Wulmar's farmstead. Wulmar took Wulwin, who was in a highly troubled and anxious state, to a monk at the local abbey who was reputed to be skilled as a healer. The monk told him, 'You have a surplus of blood humour, an excessively sanguine temperament. You must pray to Our Lady, St Mary the Virgin, that the balance of your humours be remedied and your sight restored.'

Wulwin took the monk at his word. From that day, he began a long, arduous and courageous pilgrimage. He travelled on foot from church to church, by Roman paved roads, by ancient track-ways, and over trackless downs. Unable to see the way before him, he relied upon the kindness of strangers to set him upon the right path. Walking over the downs, he relied on the direction of the sun's warmth upon his face and neck to guide him.

Arriving at each church, he told the priest of his purpose, then knelt before the altar, remaining there praying and fasting for several hours. He prayed constantly to Our Lady that she may deign to calm his sanguine temperament and restore his sight, so he might return to his work in the forest.

For the length of a year he travelled, through Oxfordshire, Wiltshire and Berkshire. The story of Wulwin the blind pilgrim became widely known, and wherever he travelled folk cared for him and gave him food and drink, and somewhere to lay his head. Being especially devoted to Our Lady, he sought out her sanctuaries: St Mary's Church, Speen; St Mary's Church, Beenham; St Mary's Church, Streatley; St Mary's Church, Reading; St Mary's Church, Thatcham; and many more.

During his pilgrimage, he visited eighty-seven churches, kneeling in prayer to Our Lady. All was in vain, yet Wulwin was never disheartened. After visiting the eighty-seventh church, the wood-built Saxon minster at Thatcham dedicated to Mary the Virgin, he had a dream as he slept on a bed of straw in a farmer's barn; he was told by the Holy Virgin that King Edward alone could heal his blindness.

Awakening from his dream, he rose from his bed of straw and set out at once on the road to Windsor, where he sat at the door of the royal palace amongst a jostling crowd of supplicants. Wulwin waited for a long time to gain admission to the King's presence, but the King was known to be a good-natured man who would turn no one away without hearing their supplication.

At last, the King sent for Wulwin, and asked to hear the story of his dream. After he had heard it he mildly answered, 'By my Lady, St Mary, I shall be truly grateful if God, through my means, shall please to take pity upon a wretched creature,' for he denied any power in himself to perform miracles. However, at the urging of his servants, who brought him a bowl of holy water, the King dipped his fingers in the bowl and placed them upon the head of the blind man.

Behold! As was accounted true by all who saw it, in a moment the blood dripped plentifully from Wulwin's eyes, and the man, restored to sight, exclaimed with rapture, 'I see you, O King! I see you, O King!'

Who could doubt? For all who saw swore it to be the truth, that on the very same day, and with the very same holy water, three blind men and a man with one eye, all of whom were graciously supported with the royal alms, received a cure; the servants who administered the healing water – which had been touched by the king – doing so with perfect confidence.

St Mary's prediction having been fulfilled, Wulwin was able to return to work in the forest – but no longer as a humble woodcutter. He was rewarded with the post of custodian of the royal forest of Windsor and controller of the royal palace.

Who can forbear to cheer at such a touching tale?

After this, many legends sprang up about Edward the Confessor, which confirm without question his reputation as a man marked out by God for sainthood. Indeed, one legend has Wulwin Spillecorn wandering from church to church not for one year but for all of seventeen years, before the saintly king healed his blindness with a light touch of his hands.

The Miracle of the Ring

For the remainder of his life, these legends of the blessed character of the King continued to accrue. One which has stood the test of time occurred towards the end of his life: the miraculous tale of King Edward's ring.

King Edward was attending the dedication of a Saxon church at Speen in honour of St John the Evangelist. The church was close to a pagan well[9] whose waters were believed from ancient times to heal eye diseases and other ills. Now, the curing of Wulwin's blindness brought forth a new belief: superior healing powers were shown to be invested by God in a pious and humble Christian sovereign.

After the ceremony, a poor man approached the King and begged him for alms, 'Alms, for the love of St John the Evangelist!' Finding neither silver nor gold in his purse, and with his almoner lost in the crowd, the King was distressed that he had nought to offer the poor beggar. Then, he bethought the princely ring upon his finger. He promptly removed the large, jewel-encrusted ring and gave it to the man, who still knelt before him. The beggar thanked the King with gentle speech and disappeared.

That same night, in faraway Palestine, two English pilgrims lost their way. The sun soon set behind the bare mountains, and the men were alone in the wilderness, knowing not where to find shelter from robbers and wild beasts.

The pilgrims were casting about, not knowing which way to turn, when there appeared before them a band of youths in bright raiment, and, in their midst, an old man, white and hoary, and wonderful to gaze upon.

'Dear friends, whence come you?' the old man asked the pilgrims, 'Of what creed and birth are you? Of what kingdom and what king? What seek you?'

'We are Christians, from England,' they replied, 'come to expiate our sins, seeking the holy places where Jesus lived and died. Our king is named Edward. And we have lost our way.'

The old man told them, 'I am John the Evangelist. For the love of Edward, I will not fail you, and you shall arrive safe and sound in England. Then, go to Edward, and say you have brought a precious ring which he gave to me at the dedication of my church, when I besought him in poor array, and tell him that in six months he shall come to me in Paradise.'

The pilgrims came back to England without misadventure, and returned the ring to Edward with the message from St John the Evangelist. When the King learned he was soon to die, he gave away all his money to those who were in need, and spent his last days this side of Paradise in prayer and devotion.

Edward the Confessor was the first Anglo-Saxon, and the only King of England, to be canonised. He was raised to the Blessed Congregation of the Just by Pope Alexander III. Surely, this was a just tribute to his reputation as an unworldly, saintly, pious and devoted servant of God and his Church.

SOURCES

Goodchild, W., 'Fragments of Local Legends and History', 1878

Verney, Margaret M., *Bucks Biographies: A School Book*, 1912

Dearmer, Percy, *The Little Lives of the Saints*, 1900

DONNINGTON CASTLE

Returning to the wagonette, we crossed the main road and travelled on through the village of Speen, turning north-east to Donnington and the ruins of Donnington Castle in the parish of Shaw-cum-Donnington. The castle was demolished during the Civil War, and around this time King Charles stopped at Shaw House. He was dressing at the window when an optimistic Roundhead fired a musket at him, missing the King but making a hole in the wainscot which can be seen to this day.

The house was bought by the 1st Duke of Chandos, but our next tale was the strange romance of the 2nd Duke, who, according to Mr Rowland, bought his wife.

THE DUKE OF CHANDOS BUYS A WIFE

'Phaa, phaa!' said King George, with his customary eloquence. 'Phaa, phaa, the man's a hot-headed, passionate, half-witted coxcomb, phaa, phaa.' He was referring to Henry Brydges, 2nd Duke of Chandos. Well, we shall see, dear listener, whether you concur with His Royal Highness' appraisal.

Henry Brydges had recently inherited the title from his father, James Brydges, 1st Duke of Chandos, along with a splendid Elizabethan mansion, Shaw House, in the parish of Shaw-cum-Donnington, near Newbury.

One day, Henry Brydges was returning to Shaw House from the Palace of Westminster in his Berline carriage, newly acquired from the capital city of Brandenburg. He was well pleased with himself and with the Berline. It was a light, four-wheeled, four-in-hand travelling carriage, far faster and more stable than the family's old coach. It had two facing bench seats and a separate hooded rear seat for his footman. The Berline's upholstered seats and newfangled leather-braced suspension afforded him a comfortable ride. Drawn by four elegant Arabian greys, Henry Brydges' Berline was a majestic sight as it progressed through the streets of Newbury.

Passing the Pelican Inn, the Duke noticed a commotion in the inn yard, and, having an inquisitive nature – not to say hot-headed and passionate – he rapped for the coachman to stop. Entering the inn yard, he saw a rough-looking man beating a young woman on the back with a cudgel. Her face was already badly bruised and she had a deep cut over her blackened left eye. She had a halter round her neck, and when the man stopped beating her he pulled her round the inn yard by the halter, shouting, 'What'll you gi' me for this fine piece o' baggage, my so-called wife. Who'll start the biddin'?'

The Duke appraised the situation – and the young woman – then strode purposefully up to the rough-looking man, and, looking down his nose at him, said in a loud and imperious tone, 'What's going on here?'

'What's it to thee?' answered the man with a savage snarl.

'You'll answer my question, my man, or I'll have you given a good thrashing,' bellowed the Duke. The Duke's coachman and footman had quietly come and stood either side of him, the coachman eagerly fingering his horsewhip.

The man squared his shoulders and retorted hotly, 'I'm selling my baggage of a wife,' then launched into a well-practised litany of her ills, 'Tha sees, my lord, she's –'

The Duke cut him off sharply, 'I'm not interested in your wife's shortcomings or misdemeanours. I'm willing to accept fifty guineas here and now to take her off your hands.'

The man was nonplussed for a moment, then, 'Di'n't you 'ear? I'm trying to sell 'er. If tha don' wan' to bid fer her tha can clear off and tek thy henchmen wi' thee.'

The Duke laughed. 'Bid for her? Bid for her? Why, if the likes of you are getting rid of her what's the merchandise worth? You'd be lucky to sell her to a tinker for a bent pot.'

The man stared truculently at the Duke, his shoulders hunched, not knowing what to say. The Duke looked down at him, thoughtfully. 'I'll tell you what, I'm a generous man after all. I'll make an offer for her, but first I must look at her teeth.'

The man was again flabbergasted, exclaiming, ''er teeth?'

'Of course her teeth,' said the Duke. 'You led her round by the halter, so I'll treat her like I would buying a horse. I'll examine her teeth.' Then, addressing the wife, 'Open wide girl.' Grabbing her jaw and forehead in his large hands, carefully avoiding the cut and bruised eye, he gently prised open her mouth and peered inside.

'See this, see this?' the Duke roared to the crowd in the inn yard. 'This fair filly has two missing front teeth, knocked out by this scoundrel I reckon, and another badly chipped. She's sorely beaten and bruised about the back and buttocks and physiognomy. She'll happen be fit for the dray or the plough.'

Grasping the halter, the Duke launched into a Dutch auction, 'Who'll bid me fifty guineas for this jenny?'

'No!' roared the crowd.

'Who'll bid me thirty guineas?'

'No!' roared the crowd. The rough-looking man looked on with mounting rage and fury, closely watched by the coachman and footman.

The Duke was enjoying himself, 'No one'll bid thirty guineas for this fine jennet? Then how about ten guineas?'

'No!' roared the crowd even more loudly, delighted at the spectacle.

'Five guineas?'

'No! No!'

The Duke gently removed the halter from around the young woman's neck. He turned to the man, cast the halter about his neck, and tossed a half guinea piece at his feet, 'Here's half a guinea for her. Now, be off before I set the horsewhip to you.'

The man grudgingly bent to pick up the coin and clumped off to swallow his humiliation in the inn.

Henry Brydges led the woman by the arm to the Berline as the footman opened the door and lowered the footstool. Henry handed the woman into the carriage and followed her inside. They sat facing one another on the upholstered seats as the carriage drew away from the inn.

The young woman looked Henry in the face, her eyes sharp despite the bruising, and spoke for the first time, 'Tha don' own me, nor will thee; not for 'alf a guinea, nor fifty guineas neither, no more than did that brute of a 'usband. And I'll not 'ave thee tek advantage o' me neither. I'm an 'onest chambermaid I am, an' I can mek mysel' useful wherever tha's tekin' me, but I'll have no 'anky panky.'

Henry replied softly, 'My name is Henry Brydges, ma'am. I deeply regret the humiliation you have suffered today, and my part in it. From henceforth you shall be treated with respect by me and my servants. We are going now to my home, Shaw House.'

The woman said her name was Ann Wells, then turned her attention to the carriage, never having ridden in a carriage before. She felt the monogrammed fabric of the seats, the sway of the coachwork on the uneven road. She studied the hoods which could be pulled down over the windows in poor weather; listened to the trotting hooves of the greys and the occasional whip crack; watched the landscape swiftly slipping by. She paid no attention to the Duke.

When they reached Shaw House, Henry led Ann through the arched entrance and escorted her, eyes wide with wonder, as they wandered from room to sumptuous room. A particular delight for her was the Chinese wallpaper on the walls of the splendid new dining room, set into plasterwork frames. She giggled with amazement, in a little side room, at the extraordinary, newfangled flush toilet. She insisted on pulling the chain several times, watching the water cascade into the bowl then listening to the cistern refilling.

On entering the house, Henry had asked Violet, his favourite chambermaid, to prepare a room for Ann. Now, he asked Violet to escort Ann to her room, to tend to her wounds, to provide her with food, and to find a nightdress for her and clean clothes for the morning. Then he bade her goodnight.

When Violet called Ann for breakfast, she found, set out in the dining room, oatmeal with sweet cream, smoked herrings, grilled trout with white butter sauce, grilled kidneys and bacon, fresh bread with butter and a choice of Berkshire honey, orange marmalade, and raspberry jam, and a large pot of tea. The centrepiece of the breakfast table was a fresh pineapple, grown in a greenhouse on the Shaw House estate.

Henry rose from the table, as Ann hesitated in the doorway, and invited her to join him for breakfast. Over breakfast, Henry suggested he promote Violet to be Ann's maid for an extra sixpence a week, and spoke about dressmakers, milliners and hairdressers, until Ann felt completely bemused. Yesterday she was being beaten and humiliated by a brutish husband, and today she was being treated like she had seen great ladies treated, and did not – dared not – believe this sudden change in her fortunes, lest it be as quickly snatched away.

Henry suggested that she write a note to the dressmaker that very morning to arrange for her to visit. She stared at him; then, dropping her eyes, she told him in a small voice that she had learnt neither to read nor to write. 'Then,' he said gently, 'I shall write for you, and I shall employ tutors for you.'

She learnt quickly, and was soon working her way through the Shaw House library. She chortled over Samuel Pepys' diary and Henry Fielding's *Tom Jones*; she was fascinated to read Captain Charles Johnson's *A General History of the Robberies and Murders of the Most Notorious Pirates*, and the exploits of *Robinson Crusoe* by Daniel Defoe; she absorbed John Bunyan's *Pilgrim's Progress* with a serious frown. Moreover, education and good conversation at the dinner table with guests took the edge off her Berkshire burr.

Henry soon found in Ann what her useless husband was never equipped to appreciate. As well as having a sharp tongue, behind her sharp eyes there was a sharp mind, a ready wit and a willingness to speak her thoughts. Moreover, with her wounds healed, and being now carefully groomed and attired, everyone could see what Henry had seen in the inn yard: that she was a beautiful and graceful woman.

The more Ann learnt about the workings of the house and estate, the more Henry conferred with her about his plans for developing the farms and greenhouses, and exploiting the timber and peat on his lands. Henry relied on Ann more and more during his frequent absences on state business, and in time she virtually became the chatelaine of Shaw House.

Yet, she never forgot her humble origins and her change in fortune, and though she was now in charge of the servants she also made friends with them. Sometimes, they felt the sharp edge of her tongue, yet they respected her because they knew she was simply being straight with them and held no rancour or malice.

Meanwhile, without Ann, the life of Ann's husband had gone to wreck. With the taunts and jeers of his fellows keeping his humiliation fresh, he had given himself over to drinking and brawling. Then one day news came to Ann at Shaw House that her husband had died in a drunken brawl.

Henry listened whilst Ann spoke to him of the good times at the start of her marriage, and she grieved a little. Then he asked her to marry him. He told her he had loved her from the moment he first saw her, beaten and bleeding, with a halter around her neck, in the yard of the Pelican Inn. She agreed to marry him, but not at St Mary's parish church in Shaw-cum-Donnington. She feared her husband's family might interrupt the reading of the banns or the marriage service itself.

So, Henry arranged for them to marry on Christmas Day at Revd Alexander Keith's Marriage Shop at May Fair, famous for its clandestine connubial contracts. But this was no hole-in-a-corner coupling, for the Duke and his bride invited some illustrious guests. The dashing young Joshua Reynolds and his friend Augustus Keppel, who sailed to sea at the age of ten, told tales of the sea and sang sea shanties; Henry Fielding entertained the party with unrepeatable jokes; Samuel Johnson and William Hogarth fenced with razor-sharp satirical wits; George Handel even played a tune or two.

On their way home to Shaw House in the Berline, Henry said to Ann, 'Well, my dove, how do you like being a duchess?'

She replied, with a coquettish elbow in his ribs, and resorting to her Berkshire burr, 'Well, ma duck, I'll let tha know int' mornin'.' And so she did.

So, I appeal to you, what is your appraisal of Henry Brydges, 2nd Duke of Chandos? Do you go along with King George that he was hot-headed? Passionate? Half-witted? A coxcomb?

SOURCE

Morris, W.A.D., *A History of the Parish of Shaw-cum-Donnington*, 1969

❧

Visit Donnington Castle. Visit Shaw House – open most weekends and some school holidays.

The bare bones of the story: Henry Brydges, 2nd Duke of Chandos (possibly before he inherited the title, while he still bore the courtesy title Marquis of Caernarfon), saw a man trying to sell his wife, a chambermaid called Ann Wells, in an inn yard. He bought her, took her to live at Shaw House in Shaw-cum-Donnington, and subsequently married her at Keith's Chapel, Mayfair on Christmas Day 1774.

❧

THIRTEEN

BOXFORD

From Donnington, we travelled north across Snelsmore Common and then turned west, following signs to Boxford, where we stopped at The Bell for some much-needed refreshment. Here Mr Vanderpump introduced us to Mr Monk, one of his correspondents, who took us to a little thatched cottage by a bridge over the River Lambourn and told us the story of the Cunning Man who once lived there.

THE WIZARD OF BOXFORD

Storyteller

A lot has been said about Berkshire's 'cunning men'. Some call them charlatans, rogues, tricksters; others believe them to be powerful wizards. Well, that's as may be; I can only speak for one 'Cunning Man', John Palmer of Boxford. I knew him as a very old man. I visited his home many times here at Brook Cottage, a pretty place with the brook flowing by, and I'm going to tell you his tale just as he told it to me:

John Palmer, the Cunning Man of Boxford

Yes, people call me a wizard (or something worse), but to start with it was just a knack I had. The first time it happened, the old widow woman who lived next door told me she'd lost her locket with her mother's likeness in it. I sat her down in my cottage, spoke gently to her, calmed her down, and told her the locket would turn up.

We sat for a few minutes, talking quietly together about where she might have put the locket, when I saw words – as if they just rose up out of the air: 'The locket is behind the toby jug on the mantelshelf.' I sat up with a jolt – I thought I must have been dreaming – then I grabbed my quill pen, dipped it in the inkwell, and wrote down the words before I forgot them. I took the old lady back to her cottage and told her she might look behind the toby jug, not believing for a moment that the locket would be there, but it was. She was amazed. So was I.

I lived in Welford then, and in no time the old widow woman had told the whole village what a clever wizard I was. After that, whenever anyone lost something, they would ask the wizard to find it. People sought me out from far and wide, even as far away as Reading.

The more I used my knack for finding things the better I got. I would sit a person down by the table in my cottage, with my quill pen and inkwell before me, and we would talk calmly about the object they had lost until they became very relaxed, their eyelids drooped, and they appeared to sleep – though afterwards they still remembered what had happened. If they were too troubled to relax, I would speak gently about the soft breeze in the trees, the cooling streams, the sound of bees around the cowslips in the meadow, until all their tension drained away. I found that as they became more relaxed and calm I became more focused on the lost object, until the words rose up out of the air and I could immediately write them down. Then, I would gently wake them up and give them the paper telling them where they could find what was lost.

I know people call me a wizard or a Cunning Man[10], but I call myself an extologer – like an astrologer, except I read words rising out of the air rather than reading the stars.

When I was sitting with one of these visitors one evening, the curfew bell – hung in the round Norman church tower – began to toll. I was concentrating very hard on a lost wedding ring, and I reckon I didn't want my visitor to be disturbed, so without knowing I was doing it I snapped my fingers and the bell stopped ringing right away. I just carried on helping my visitor to find her ring. After that, whenever the curfew bell began to toll while I was with a visitor, I would snap my fingers to stop it. I didn't think much about it; it seemed so trivial next to extology.

Well, it turned out that Squire Jones, who lived in a fine manor house, Welford Park – built in the reign of Queen Anne, hard by the church tower – liked his supper served promptly when the curfew bell tolled. When I stopped the bell tolling almost as soon as it started (and sometimes before it started), Squire Jones didn't get his dinner. When hunger pains began to gnaw at his stomach, he stormed into the kitchen and laid about his servants with a horsewhip. He was not a patient man, not one to listen to explanations, and none too bright neither, but eventually he cottoned on that it was me what stopped the curfew bell and delayed his supper, so it was me what got the whipping along with a lot of threats.

Well, extology and my visitors were a sight more important to me than an ill-tempered squire with addled wits, so I just carried on stopping the bell when I needed to. That is, until he turned up on my doorstep with his cronies. They dragged me out of my cottage, and two of his brutes lifted me by the arms while the others pulled off my breeches. With the whole community gathered to watch, I was horse-whipped out of the village in my drawers with their drop flap hanging open, only too painfully aware of my disgrace.

Clear of the village, I buttoned up my drop flap and made for Wickham, intending to put up at the Five Bells, where I ran into a couple of drovers on a delivery to their employer, Squire Jones. They made some quite unseemly and ribald remarks about my state of dress. They were too much in their cups for fisticuffs, so I fixed them with a stare and after a while told them, 'In the morning you'll not be able to rise until I allow it, then you'll travel on to Welford without your breeches, with the drop flap of your drawers hanging open.' I didn't know if this would work, but it did, with the confused drovers the butt of scatological humour all the way. Squire Jones was apoplectic with rage at this insult. Storming into my abandoned cottage, he seized my one and only grimoire – *The Marvellous Mysteries of Natural Magic* by Petit Albert – purchased at great cost, and burnt the book on the village green. Ah well!

I made my way to Boxford, where I found my reputation for extology had gone before me, so I was able to carry on my work in peace. As I'd left all my worldly wealth at Welford, my patrons, as I now called them, made me small rewards for helping them recover their precious possessions, and I was able to take Brook Cottage. In time, I gained a lovely wife and two beautiful daughters, who happily inherited my peculiar knack.

What a time I've had with my extology patrons, learning new skills all the time. There was James Sweetzer, from Mortimer – you may know him. After his house had been burgled, he paid me 2s to discover who'd robbed him of some nice pieces of silver.

We sat at my table, quill and ink at the ready, and spoke about how the robbers had forced a window to get in when the household was all at church, how they'd turned out every cupboard to find what they were looking for, and had made off before the cook left church early to get the lunch on. I made light responses as he talked, often just ums and ahs, to help him relax into his narrative and me to centre myself and get ready to read the words as they arose. James was shocked later to read the words which had arisen: 'Your silver is in your third footman's father's privy.'

James took his first footman, 6½ft tall and almost as broad, to retrieve the silver from the privy, hidden under a heap of coal, and apprehend the villain of the piece. It became clear that the third footman was innocent of any crime beyond being a blabbermouth, and received nothing worse than a kick up the backside, whilst his rascally father was committed to Reading Assize.

Lots of people wanted me to track down robbers after that, even some who'd not been robbed! I was almost a parish constable. But the tale what still makes me chuckle is 'The Hand of Glory'. There was this spate of robberies in Winterbourne. People in those parts got the idea the robbers used a magical candlestick called 'The Hand of Glory', so naturally I was first to be called in.

I remembered reading about 'The Hand of Glory' in my old grimoire by Petit Albert. As a hanged felon swings from the gallows tree, on a lone bleak moor at the midnight hour, his hand is severed from his corpse, along with five locks of his hair. From the

clawed hand then is made a grisly candlestick. The five locks of
hair are twisted into wicks for fingers and for thumb. Robbers in
possession of this charm can pass through locked and bolted doors
of any dwelling, in the dark of night, by chanting this spell:

Now open lock to the Dead Man's knock!
Fly bolt, and bar, and band!
Nor move, nor swerve, joint, muscle, or nerve,
At the spell of the Dead Man's hand!
Sleep all who sleep! Wake all who wake!
But be as the Dead for the Dead Man's sake!

Lord knows how it worked, but, so I was told, this put everybody in the house into a deep trance so the burglars could search for valuables and make their getaway in peace. Even when awoken by the robbers' clatter, the residents found themselves immobile, terrified, unable even to raise an eyelid.

Well, anyway, there was this rich farmer's farmhouse which hadn't been done yet, so I went along there one evening with two brawny local lads and my cunning daughters, who had a pail of milk each. Then we waited. We waited most of the night – I fair near nodded off to be honest – until we heard the knock and the chant:

Now open lock to the Dead Man's knock!
Fly bolt, and bar, and band!
Nor move, nor swerve, joint, muscle, or nerve,
At the spell of the Dead Man's hand!
Sleep all who sleep! Wake all who wake!
But be as the Dead for the Dead Man's sake!

I was awake in no time. I heard the bolts draw back, the lock click open. I saw the door swing back and the light from the dead man's hand illuminate the threshold. My daughters upped and extinguished the candle with both pails of milk. The villains dropped the hand and legged it over the fields with the two brawny lads at their heels. I never heard whether the brawny lads caught the robbers, but there were no more robberies after that and I walked away with 3s.

There were sad cases sometimes, where people had died in tragic circumstances and their spirits couldn't find their way to the next world, like little six-year-old Lucy Fennell. She and her grandmother had perished in a fire one night forty years before, and their spirits had lodged themselves in a big house near their burnt-out cottage. A new family had moved into the house and every night they heard crackling sounds like burning thatch and timbers, and their candles and oil lamps lit themselves. The family were alarmed and the children were panic-stricken and didn't want to stay in the house, so I was called in to help, though I'd done nothing quite like this before.

For a start, I just walked around all the rooms in the house. I noticed the spare bedroom felt colder than the rest, so I called the family in, adults and children alike, assured them there was nothing to fear, and we sat on the floor in a circle. I asked them to tell me in a whisper all about the burning sounds and the lights coming on, while I spoke to them softly, lots of ums and ahs, and 'you're safe to talk', and 'that's good', and 'yes, go on', until they did feel safe and lapsed into silence. Then I concentrated on that space where the writing arises, which I knew by then was somewhere in my own mind. This time it was not written words I found in the space but spoken words uttered by Lucy Fennell – a tirade against her stepfather. He had blamed Lucy's grandmother for her mother's death and had returned in the night to wreak vengeance by setting fire to the cottage before slipping silently away.

Lucy's spirit could not move on to the next world while justice was denied her in this one, and neither could she release her grandmother's spirit. My gentle coaxing was unavailing against Lucy's will to remain and see justice done. When I told her I would help her find justice, Lucy's spirit agreed not to trouble the family further, and I was able to close the circle, reassure the family and promise to return on the morrow.

The following day I asked around and found the stepfather's grave in unconsecrated ground across the River Lambourn in the hamlet of Westbrook. He had been so filled with remorse for having been the cause of Lucy's death that he had taken his own life.

I returned to the house that same evening after sunset to find the place in uproar. The lamps were constantly turning themselves on and off, and the sound and smoke of burning thatch filled the house. The family huddled together outside, the children wailing and screaming in terror. I was furious that the spirits had broken their promise to me, as I strode into the house, up the stairs and into the spare room.

Then I calmed myself, sat on the floor, and entered that inner space where words and images arise. An irate grandmother quickly emerged, shrieking, 'There can be no justice for us who have gypsy blood!' Lucy was with her, in the background, now a sad little six-year-old girl. I remained very still in my mind and murmured the tale of the stepfather's suicide. Lucy then came forward and gradually calmed her grandmother, making her understand that justice of a kind had been done.

I asked Lucy and her grandmother if they were now willing to pass on to the next world, as a shaft of bright moonlight filled the room. Lucy looked at me, smiled for the first time, a smile of gladness and gratitude, and, taking her grandmother's hand, the two rode the moonbeam to the land beyond. The room was warm now, and I was able to shepherd the family in to feel its warmth and assure them that their house was now at peace.

Storyteller

So, this tale tells you something of the quality of this Cunning Man, known as the Wizard of Boxford. Actually, I was visiting him at the time he died. He was telling me about other cunning men in Berkshire when he suddenly broke off. A look of rapture illuminated his face. He said, 'It's time for me to go. Goodbye, old friend. Open all the windows wide and let my soul fly free.' Then he was gone, save for a seraphic smile upon his lips. So I opened the windows wide and his soul soared out like a white bird.

Sources

Barham, Revd Richard H., *The Ingoldsby Legends*, 1840

Huntley, Elsie, *Boxford Barleycorn*, 1970

Reading Evening Post, 30 October 1969

Rosen, Barbara, *Witchcraft in England: 1558-1618*, 1991

There is still a Brook Cottage in Boxford, a delightful thatched cottage. The present owners tell us that it used to be called Wizard's Cottage. The wrought-iron fence panels depict a wizard's head.

FOURTEEN

KINTBURY

We continued west to Welford. Its Saxon church was rebuilt by the Normans. Forty years ago the church was demolished and rebuilt on its original Saxon foundations. The stones of the unusual round tower and spire were carefully marked before the tower was dismantled, and so carefully re-erected that you would never guess they had been moved since Saxon times.

From Welford we travelled south, through Wickham Green and across the Great West Road to Kintbury. The village was originally called Kennetbury and the church of St Mary the Virgin, an ancient building of flint, stone and brick, stands on a rise above the river.

Having stopped and looked round the church, we walked up Church Street and into High Street, stopping at the Blue Ball for a little light refreshment, while Mr Vanderpump related a Kintbury story:

THE KINTBURY BELL

Eliza Hidden was an ill-favoured, ill-tempered harridan, scrawny and scabby, with hook nose and piercing black eyes. Her mouth was a thin toothless gash enclosing a vicious tongue. She called herself a soothsayer, but the villagers of Kintbury said – to themselves, you understand, fearing her malice – 'Keep your sooth to yourself,' for much of her foretelling was doom-laden. Behind their hands the villagers dubbed Eliza Hidden the Kintbury Witch.

All the same, the villagers grudgingly consulted her when a ring was lost or a horse went lame, and always she exacted a heavy price

for her service – not in currency but in indebtedness, and by such she garnered her power.

Nobody in the village was more indebted to Eliza Hidden than a farmer, Tobias Tubb. He had suffered a series of misfortunes: a mysterious sickness blighted his flock of sheep and their lambs miscarried; his wheat withered while surrounding farms flourished; his cows' milk dried up and the cows became barren. For each of Farmer Tubb's tribulations, Eliza Hidden was ready with a remedy: a salve for the sheep, an incantation for the crops, a concoction for the cows, drawing him deeper and deeper into her debt.

Eliza's bitter rival was John Palmer, the Cunning Man of the nearby village of Boxford. Eliza knew that some of the villagers sidled off in secret to consult the so-called Wizard of Boxford when they lost a ring or a horse went lame. She hated him for encroaching on her territory and devised a plan to defeat him and wrest back her power.

The tower of Kintbury's ancient minster held a peal of four bells: the Treble tuned to D#, the Third tuned to C#, the Fifth tuned to A#, and the Tenor tuned to G#. The Tenor was called the Kintbury Great Bell. It had a 38in mouth diameter and weighed 10cwt 2qtr.

One fierce winter storm, high winds shook the old stonework of the minster's tower, creating a chaotic clanging of bells. The storm brought down part of the tower, and falling masonry crashed onto the Kintbury Bell. As the great bell cracked, a hollow, fractured tenor tolled across the village.

Later, the Kintbury Witch watched with a satisfied slit of a smile from the opposite bank as the Tenor bell was carefully loaded and lashed onto a pontoon for transport up the River Kennet to the Aldbourne Foundry for repair.

She was there again when the repaired bell was returned on its pontoon – with sly looks, muttering to herself, conjuring mischief. At the moment the great bell was being unloaded onto the bank, there was a sudden turbulence in the water. The villagers on the bank watched with dismay as the pontoon gradually tipped and the Kintbury Great Bell slid serenely into the depths. With a complacent smirk and a dismissive toss of the head, Eliza Hidden turned and skipped away.

In the days and weeks following, many attempts were made by the villagers to heave the bell from the water. Each time, Eliza Hidden watched from the opposite bank, a malevolent sneer on her ravaged countenance. Each attempt failed. As the bell sank ever deeper into the river mud, Eliza's malicious grin grew ever wider, her leaps of delight ever higher. Some villagers even appealed to her for help, but she dismissed them with a brusque wave of her bony hand.

Finally, two of the village elders were sent to Boxford by donkey cart to seek help from the wizard. He sat them down by the table in his cottage, his quill pen and inkwell before him. He talked with them calmly about the sinking of the Kintbury Bell, until they became more relaxed, their eyelids drooped, and they appeared to sleep.

The wizard murmured to them about the gentle flow of the River Kennet and the soft breeze in the willows by its banks, until all their tension drained away.

As they became more relaxed and calm, he became more focused on the sunken bell, until he saw words arise out of the air. He immediately wrote them down, then gently woke up his visitors and gave them the paper with these words, telling them what they must do:

One midnight of bright silver stars, when the moon is full,
A new chain shall be threaded through the argent of the bell.
To this chain tie the traces of twelve oxen in a row.
The oxen shall be as white as newly fallen snow.
Twelve maids in white, each with a blood-red sash,
Shall lead the oxen with a silken lash,
Who, wielding their whips of silken thong,
Shall drive the oxen silently along.
While from the depths the Kintbury Bell is drawn,
No one shall speak a word, nor sneeze, nor cough, nor groan,
But shall be as mute and silent as carved stone.
Or else, the sacred charm will break in twain,
Then you will never see the bell again,
And all your hope, heartache, and cost will be in vain.

The villagers set to with renewed will and vigour. The cattlemen sought out twelve pure-white Berkshire oxen for the farrier to shoe. Because an ox cannot easily balance on three legs whilst the fourth is shod, the farrier would throw the ox to the ground and lash all four feet to a heavy wooden tripod until the shoeing was complete. As oxen have cloven hooves, each hoof was shoed with a symmetrical pair of half-moon-shaped shoes, to which the farrier fitted calkins for better traction.

The saddler made large horse-collars for the oxen. He reckoned these gave more pulling power than yokes. He made the collars flexible enough to follow the animals' movements by fitting each collar with leather pads for shoulders and neck, the three points where power is applied. Twelve maidens were chosen to lead the oxen. A seamstress made them plain white gowns with blood-red sashes and gave them whips of silken thong. Now, all was ready to recover the tower's Tenor bell.

Meanwhile, Eliza Hidden had been about her own mischievous and crafty work. She met Tobias Tubb in secret and offered to wipe out his entire debt in return for a trifling favour, or else he would see a tenfold compounding of his misfortunes.

It was midnight. The stars shone brightly with a silvery light. The moon was full. A brave farmhand dived into the River Kennet and threaded a new bright chain through the argent of the bell. The chain was attached to the traces of the twelve well-shod oxen, white as newly fallen snow, each attended by a pretty maid in a plain white gown with a blood-red sash.

The entire village watched, with never a word, nor sneeze, nor cough, nor groan, as the maids guided their oxen with their silken lashes. The row of oxen slowly and steadily moved forward. The Kintbury Bell ever so gradually lifted from the mud until it broke the surface of the dark water. Guided by the maidens, the oxen continued to move forward at a steady pace until the bell was on the very brink of tipping onto the bank.

At that moment, a wild shout broke the silence, 'Here again comes Kintbury's Great Bell. In spite of all the devils in Hell!' Instantly, the bright new chain snapped asunder and the great bell plunged back into the depths. Tobias Tubb had cleared his indebtedness to the Kintbury Witch.

Eliza Hidden was on the opposite bank, hopping and skipping and leaping and dancing around with glee, her face split wide in a toothless grin of triumph. She had prevailed over her rival, the Wizard of Boxford. The scowling and disconsolate villagers turned away and returned to their cottages.

The following morning, all forlorn, the two village elders returned to Boxford in the donkey cart to tell the wizard what had transpired. He soothed them with his gentle words, then sat in silent thought for a long time before speaking. 'You've probably heard the tale. When I lived in Welford I found I could silence the curfew bell. I was sitting with a patron who had lost her wedding ring when the curfew bell began to toll. Not wishing my patron to be disturbed, I thoughtlessly snapped my fingers and the bell stopped ringing right away. Now I'm thinking, if one bell can be silenced, another bell can be made to sound.' Then he told them what was to be done.

The village elders returned to Kintbury in good spirits. They gathered together the bell ringers in the ringing room below the minster tower. They asked the ringers of the Treble, Third, and Fifth bells to stand by their bell ropes, and the ringer of the Tenor

bell to stand on the box where his rope would hang. Then they
asked the band to ring rounds: Treble – Third – Fifth – Tenor.
Each time he pulled his imaginary rope, the ringer of the Tenor
was to recall the resonance and affinity he felt for his bell. In
support, as they heard the rounds, the whole community was
to imagine the Tenor bell sounding in their ears. The ringing of
rounds began:

Treble D#
      Third C#
            Fifth A#
                  Silence

Treble D#
      Third C#
            Fifth A#
                  Silence

Treble D#
      Third C#
            Fifth A#
                  Silence …

… until the bell ringers and the village elders began to hear a faint
sound from the river, getting louder all the time.

Treble D#
      Third C#
            Fifth A#
                  Tenor G#

Treble D#
      Third C#
            Fifth A#
                  Tenor G#

Treble D#
     Third C#
          Fifth A#
               Tenor G# …

The moment had come for the village elders to ask the bell ringers to ring the changes of a Plain Hunt. Then, the full power of the Kintbury Great Bell rang out from the river:

Treble D#
     Third C#
          Fifth A#
               Tenor G#

Third C#
     Treble D#
          Tenor G#
               Fifth A#

Third C#
     Tenor G#
          Treble D#
               Fifth A# …

Once more the Kintbury Great Bell was the Bourdon Bell of the peal, the one with the lowest pitch. The villagers rushed from their cottages when they heard the full peal of bells. They stood and listened with wonder at the sound of the Kintbury Bell tolling from the depths of the River Kennet. Then, with joy in their hearts, and good ale and a fine feast in their bellies, all the villagers celebrated the return of the Kintbury Great Bell, even shamefaced Tobias Tubb. All save Eliza Hidden, the Kintbury Witch. She was consumed by bitter rage, trounced at the last by John Palmer, the Wizard of Boxford.

SOURCES

Westwood, Jennifer and Simpson, Jacqueline, *The Lore of the Land*, 2006
Sharpe, Frederick, *The Church Bells of Berkshire*, 1970

෨

The bare bones of the story: In one account, it is said that the Kintbury Bell rolled into the river when the tower collapsed in a storm; in another, it is said that the bell fell into the water while being returned by river after a repair.

When all efforts to recover the bell failed, a local wizard was consulted. He advised the villagers to raise it in silence using a new chain, oxen, maidens, and silken thongs. At the critical moment, the voice of the Kintbury Witch, or a person bewitched by her, cried out, and the bell fell back into the depths, irretrievably. Afterwards, when the bells were in full peal, the Kintbury Bell could still be heard, the bell with the lowest pitch (or Bourdon Bell).

When you visit St Mary's, Kintbury's parish church, you will find there are now six bells in the belfry, and you can read about the addition of the two newest bells, and the refurbishment and blessing of the bells and ringing chamber.

෨

FIFTEEN

HUNGERFORD

As the sun waned, we took the road that lies to the south of the Kennet to Hungerford, where we were booked to spend the night at the Three Swans Hotel, on the High Street opposite the Town Hall. The main street is broad, and after dinner we walked up one side and down the other before crossing the river and exploring the lower part of the town, ending up in the bar of the Bear Hotel. Here we sat talking about our day's journey. At the mention of the Blue Ball in Kintbury, an old man in the inglenook, clay pipe clutched in one hand and pint pot beside him, looked up and called to us, 'I've a tale to tell, if you've a mind to hear it.'

We gathered round him and urged him to tell his tale.

CAPTAIN SWING RIOTS – 'BREAD OR BLOOD'

'When I was ten years old, I went with my mother and my two little sisters to see my father in Reading Gaol. I'm going to tell you the tale he told to me and my mother, as she wept and he bounced his little daughters on his knees. I will begin with the tale his father told to him.'

The Grandfather's Tale

Our family had lived and worked on this land near Hungerford since ancient times, long before there was any notion of land ownership or title. The land was common to all of us, as villagers, and we worked on it together. Trouble was, though we cherished these ancient unwritten rights, we had no title.

Our horses, cows and sheep grazed on our common pasture. We collected firewood from the woods and copses to fuel our stove. On the arable part of our common we had a six-year rotation of crops. In the first year we grew wheat; the second barley; the third oats with seeds; the fourth clover, mowed and then grazed in common; the fifth oats or barley; the sixth year we left the land fallow. We each had a strip of land from which we took our portion of the crop. Some years the living was meagre, other years were plentiful, but we could feel content, following the cycle of the seasons.

Then, in 1811, our troubles began. We were dispossessed of our common land. It was taken from us, enclosed by an Act of Parliament which described enclosure as 'extinguishing village communities'. There were wealthy landowners in the Hungerford area, men who did have title to their lands. They used their wealth to make bargains with the Enclosure Commissioners to trample upon our traditional rights and take our common land from us.

The times were bad for me and my family. Some folk were compensated for the loss of their rights, with an allotment of one acre of land, but the Enclosure Commissioners reckoned our mean little cottage had been built by squatters so we had no title and got no compensation. This meant we had nowhere for our animals to graze, so we had to sell them for the little they could raise. The loss of our common meant we could no longer collect wood to fuel our stove, making life very difficult.

Working the common had never provided enough, so I had also worked for Tom Tull, whose farm lay next to the common, paid partly in kind and partly in cash. He had added to his farm all the land that had been our common, and now my only income was what I earned working for him. Up till then, I was on a one-year contract, but when it ended he would only re-hire me on a one-month cash-only contract. Monthly contracts meant he could reduce my wages whenever he liked. In the end he only hired me on a weekly contract on poor wages. He reckoned the Poor Law relief would make up the difference, which, of course, it never did.

A further burden was added; we had to pay a tithe to support the Church of England parson. Previously, 10 per cent of our harvest went into the tithe barn to support the clergyman's living. Now, we were made to pay a firmly enforced cash sum, far more than we could afford, regardless of whether we were Church or Chapel, to pay the parson a generous wage.

These were harsh times for us. Within a few years we had suffered dispossession of our common land, denial of compensation, progressive impoverishment, and the imposition of crippling cash tithes.

The Father's Tale

There were poor harvests in 1829 and 1830, causing a rise in the price of bread and in unemployment among rural labourers. Father and me were laid off during the bitter winter months from our work on Tom Tull's farm.

On top of all the suffering my father described, we faced a new threat when farmers started bringing in horse-powered threshing machines. During the months after the harvest was gathered in, we had stayed in work to do the threshing. Now, when our one-week contract finished after harvest, we were laid off and had no wages coming in. We had Poor Law relief, but each person needed 3½ gallon loaves[11] each week to keep body and soul together, and the Poor Law only gave us enough money for two loaves. We starved.

Then, one day, these big tough men arrived from Kent, with their angry and powerful words. They told us about their leader, Captain Swing, who was stirring up protests against the poor living conditions of agricultural workers – the 'oppressed poor' they called us. This Captain Swing wrote letters to the landed gentry – opulent landowners, farmers, magistrates and clergymen – demanding an end to starvation wages. When there was no response, Captain Swing called on the workers to riot, with the slogan 'Bread or Blood'.

Well, the condition of us agricultural workers in the villages around Hungerford was no better than in Kent. Since the enclosure of our common land, things had gone from bad to worse, as my father has described, and now the new threshing machines were reducing the need for our labour.

So, the words of the Kent men made a powerful impact on us, 'Bread or Blood'. Their words worked like fire in a hayrick, internal combustion slowly warming up until the whole rick burst into flame. Once it starts, there is no damping it down.

Captain Swing letters were written to all the landed gentry. We knew by this time that 'Captain Swing' was just a made-up name, to protect the letter writers. The letters had an effect, though. The gentry was worked up, fearful about what had happened in Kent: rioters burning tithe barns, demanding money with menaces, wrecking threshing machines.

The gentry called a Vestry Meeting right away and agreed an increase to our agricultural wages, from 9s to 10s per week, and an increase to Poor Law relief, for a married man with more than two children, by the cost of an extra gallon loaf for each child above his second.

Meanwhile, a crowd of us had gathered outside Hungerford Town Hall to give support to our demands. John Willes, a county magistrate, met our spokesmen, which included me. He told us about the increases the Vestry Meeting had agreed, to which we gave our assent.

Mr Willes then complimented the conduct of the rural labourers, which, he said, was marked by restraint and civility in the way we expressed our sense of the suffering and hardship we had endured and our repudiation of any intention to provoke riot or disorder.

We left the Town Hall intending to tell the crowd of the increases which had been agreed and to ask them to disperse, but this proved impossible. By that time, the Hungerford men had been joined by the Kintbury mob, who were in an angry and rebellious mood. They had already smashed the windows of Mr Anning's house, and at Richard Gibbons' Iron Foundry they had destroyed his stock and machinery.

The Kintbury mob sent in a deputation to meet Mr Willes – William Oakley, William Winterbourne, Daniel Bates and Edmund Steel. Their spokesman, William Oakley, demanded agricultural wages of 2s 6d a day and £5 in cash there and then, 'Or we'll be damned if we don't smash up this place and the whole of Hungerford.'

Mr Willes handed over five sovereigns to get rid of them, but, by the time the mob had spent the money on liquor, righteous anger had spilled over into drunken rage.

The mob stopped the Bath and London coaches. They broke the windows and extorted money from the passengers. Then, they went into the villages, demanding money from landowners with threats (some of which they carried out) to smash threshing machinery.

Finally, Job Hanson, a much respected Kintbury stonemason and Wesleyan Methodist district preacher, managed to quieten the mob, restore peace, and send the rioters to their beds.

The peace was not to last. The next day, the labourers of West Woodhay, Enborne, Welford, Boxford, West Shefford and Hampstead Marshall heard of the money given to the Kintbury labourers. They formed a mob and descended on the Kintbury men's meeting place, the Blue Ball, persuading them to join in another round of rioting and destruction.

Within a couple of days, 300 special constables had been sworn in at Hungerford. Led by Colonel Dundas, these 'gentlemen on horseback' proceeded to round up those they saw as leading the rioting. This included William Oakley, William Winterbourne, Daniel Bates and Edmund Steel from Kintbury. It also included me and other Hungerford spokesmen, even though we were guilty of nothing except, in Mr Willes' words, restraint and civility in the way we expressed our sense of the suffering and hardship we had endured and our repudiation of any intention to provoke riot or disorder.

But innocence was no defence against a mob formed of landed gentry and magistrates determined to inflict severe punishment on the class of rural labourers, the oppressed poor. I reckon this genteel mob was as driven by fear as we were. We feared starvation. But, following what had happened in France, the gentry feared for their necks.

So, here you find me, in Reading Gaol and in despair. Though innocent of any crime, I have been torn away from my family and await transfer to the prison hulks and transportation to the other side of the world.

The Son's Tale

We never saw father again. Father was well thought of, and several people were willing to petition the Home Secretary, Lord Melbourne, on his behalf. Even Tom Tull wrote a petition, saying how father was a sober, civil, diligent and reliable worker, who cared for his family and regularly attended chapel services, pointing out that without father's income the family would be destitute. But it did no good. The government was as scared of the poor and as determined to punish them as the local gentry.

Father was transported to New South Wales on the convict ship *Eleanor* on 19 February 1831. William Winterbourne was hanged.

Our lives then became even more wretched than before. Because father had been convicted, his family had to be punished as well; we were denied any Poor Law relief.

For a time we just starved, only surviving by begging and scavenging scraps of food others threw out (and, to be honest, by what I could gain by poaching and pilfering, dangerous though this was).

We didn't all survive. My two little sisters, weakened by starvation, caught the measles and died. Later, my mother managed to get a bit of farm work from Tom Tull's son. When I was twelve, I asked Job Hanson for work. He took pity on me, knowing the injustice done to my father, and I became an apprentice stonemason with bed and board. So, my mother and me, we scraped by. This is my tale.

❧

When the old man finished speaking, we sat in silence for some while, grieving for the suffering of these Berkshire folk.

Sources

Chambers, Jill, 'Berkshire machine breakers – Captain Swing and the 1830 riots', *Berkshire Family Historian*, 2000

Reading Mercury, 22 September 1956

Read, W., *John Francis Dandridge, Machine Breaker or Swing Rioter*, 2010

Slater, Gilbert, *The English Peasantry and the Enclosure of Common Fields*, 1907

Between 1811 and 1828 almost 32,000 acres of common land in Berkshire were enclosed, resulting in severe hardship to the rural poor.

In his book on enclosure, Gilbert Slater recognised the need for reform of agricultural practice, but made a telling comment on the way this was achieved:

> The policy of the legislature and of the Central Government, expressed in the Enclosure Acts of the eighteenth and nineteenth centuries, though it claimed, and on the whole rightly claimed, that it effected an immediate and great increase in the country's output of agricultural produce, and an improvement in the breeds of sheep and cattle, was nevertheless essentially a policy directed towards the enhancement of agricultural rents, the building up of large and compact landed estates, the establishment of capitalist farming, the uprooting of peasant proprietors and of small holdings together with the communal use of land, and the multiplication of the class of landless agricultural labourers.

LAMBOURN

We returned to the Three Swans with much to think about, realising that the past in rural Berkshire had not always been the peaceful and idyllic place of our imagination.

The next morning we set out early, heading north. We turned east on to the Great West Road, then north again up Eddington Hill. Crossing the Roman road known as Ermine Way, we continued to Great Shefford, a Saxon settlement originally called Sheep-ford. Here we turned left and passed the church with its octagonal tower. We went out of the village, following the southern bank of the River Lambourn past East Garston and through the delightful village of Eastbury.

As we entered Lambourn, an alehouse, aptly named The Lamb, stood before us. Here we stopped and I told a downland tale:

The Cheviot Shepherd's Charm

When his elder brother inherited the farm, Shepherd Alan quit his beloved Cumberland hills with goodwill, and with a small flock of twenty Cheviot sheep, a ram, and two wily border collies, set out for pastures new. In his slow progress, he followed the ancient drove roads and drift roads southward, where he had heard there was sweet pasture on the wide chalk downs.

Each evening he would whistle the dogs to gather the sheep, which by some inborn protectiveness packed together, circling round and round. Counting them was like counting small children on a helter-skelter, but Shepherd Alan knew each one and would slowly tick off his twenty sheep in his mind, using the way of counting sheep passed down through countless generations of shepherds before him:

Yan, tyan, tethera, methera, pip,
Sethera, lethera, hovera, dovera, dock,
Yan-a-dock, tyan-a-dock, tethera-dock, methera-dock, bumfit,
Yan-a-bumfit, tyan-a-bumfit, tethera-bumfit, methera-bumfit, giggot.

As he counted, he would think about his favourite New Testament parable: 'What man of you, having an hundred sheep, if he lose one of them, doth not leave the ninety and nine in the wilderness, and go after that which is lost, until he find it?'[12]

When his small flock was gathered in, he would lie down and slowly count the ninety and nine, twenty at a time, passing a pebble from hand to hand for each score: 'Giggot … giggot … giggot … giggot … methera-bumfit …' and then he would sleep.

Each morning he would wake at dawn and say aloud his favourite verse: 'I am the Good Shepherd; the Good Shepherd giveth his life for the sheep.'[13]

Then, he would speak the Cheviot Shepherd's Charm, to protect his sheep and all else he loved:

Yan, tyan, tethera, methera, pip,
Good Shepherd, watch my sheep.
Sethera, lethera, hovera, dovera, dock,
Good Shepherd, guard my flock.

Shepherd Alan made his home near the village of Lambourn. His flock thrived on the chalk downs and he prospered. He married a sturdy farmer's daughter, Hannah, who made a loyal and loving wife. When Goodwife Hannah got with child, Shepherd Alan was the happiest man alive.

Everyone liked Shepherd Alan and Goodwife Hannah except for Shepherd Joshua. He had known Hannah all his life and had hoped to marry her, but that interloper Shepherd Alan had lured her away. Seeing Alan and Hannah so happy together twisted Joshua's heart like a wrung floor cloth.

For all he was happy living on the downs, Shepherd Alan missed his Cumberland hills. Whenever he heard the playing of pipes, they evoked memories of the pipers down from Scotland, and how everyone would dance and sing.

So, whenever he heard the strains of a wandering piper coming over the downs, Shepherd Alan went out to greet him with a spring in his step and gave him fine ale and food and lodging, and paid him well for an evening of dancing and entertainment.

But the people of the chalk downs were suspicious of pipers and feared them. There were fairy mounds scattered over the downs, and there were tales of nights when the fairy mounds were open and all lit up and loud with the music of fairy pipers, and darker tales of folk being lured into the mounds by the People of the Hill, never to be seen again.

Though Hannah did not utter her fears for her husband, Alan saw the anxiety in her face, and, to keep all safe, he taught her the Cheviot Shepherd's Charm:

Yan, tyan, tethera, methera, pip,
Good Shepherd, watch my sheep.
Sethera, lethera, hovera, dovera, dock,
Good Shepherd, guard my flock.

In his twisted mind, Shepherd Joshua came to believe that if only he could be rid of Shepherd Alan he could step into his place beside Goodwife Hannah. So, he stole out one moonless night, with the flittermice and Jenny Howletts[14], to a bare fairy mound to tryst with the King of the People of the Hill, whom he summoned with his own downland sheep-counting shepherd's charm:

Hant, Tant, Tothery, Fothery, Fant,
King of Fairies heed my chant.
Sahny, Dahny, Downy, Dominy, Dik,
King of Fairies come here quick.

Soon after, the call of a piper drew Shepherd Alan away, and he disappeared under the hill. Goodwife Hannah suffered such distress at the loss of her husband that it brought on the birth of twin boys. When her babies were as soon whisked away by the People of the Hill, her distress turned to anguish, terror and despair.

Now was Joshua's chance to claim wife, flock and fortune. But Hannah saw into his twisted heart, and, when she uttered the Cheviot Shepherd's Charm, 'Yan, tyan, tethera, methera, pip …' his legs turned to jelly, his bowels turned to curdled custard, and he slunk away. It was the same each time he sought to woo her: she uttered the Cheviot Shepherd's Charm, 'Yan, tyan, tethera, methera, pip …' and his legs turned to jelly, his bowels turned to curdled custard, and he slunk away. And so, for seven long years, she kept the flock and fortune safe and grieved the loss of her husband and twin boys.

Being a poor hand at husbandry, Shepherd Joshua's interest settled more and more on Hannah's flock and fortune than on Hannah herself. He made sinister plans and left on a long journey. Hannah was mightily glad to be rid of him. He travelled far, scouring the land for twin orphan boys the exact age of Hannah's own, until he found Jack and Dick, living on the parish. When he offered the boys a home, the parish was glad enough to be shot of these disturbing, fey infants. But the boys were not glad, for he beat and starved them on their long journey back to the downs.

Joshua took the boys to Hannah, saying, 'I have travelled far to find your stolen twins, and here they are restored to you. Now, you will look more kindly upon me.' Hannah knew in her heart these were not her sons, but when she saw them on her doorstep, footsore and weary, their faces pinched and forlorn, their bodies bruised and thin, she took pity upon them and brought them in. But still she would not marry Joshua. When she turned to him and uttered the Cheviot Shepherd's Charm, Jack and Dick enthusiastically joined in:

> Yan, tyan, tethera, methera, pip,
> Good Shepherd, watch my sheep.
> Sethera, lethera, hovera, dovera, dock,
> Good Shepherd, guard my flock.

Hearing these words, Joshua's legs turned to jelly, his bowels turned to curdled custard, and he slunk away.

Hannah, Jack and Dick lived contentedly together. She cared for them and became their teacher and they shepherded her sheep. One day, Jack and Dick told Hannah, 'Tomorrow we must search for a lost ewe and her two lost lambs. Oh, yes, and tomorrow we shall be seven years old.'

Hannah wept when she heard this, and told them of her lost husband, and of her lost boys who would also be seven tomorrow.

'Then we shall find them for you,' they told her with a quiet assurance.

On the morrow, Jack and Dick set out long before dawn. When they found the fairy mound, by following the sound of distant music, they danced around it seven times, counting: 'Yan, tyan, tethera, methera, pip, sethera, lethera.' After seven circuits the mound opened, they heard the music more loudly, and out came the two lost boys with the lost ewe and its two lambs. 'Now there are seven of us,' they said, 'and we must arrive home before sunrise.' Hannah ran to meet the seven just as the sun was rising and wept with joy over her tow-headed sons, who had been lost and now were found. Yet, amidst her joy, her heart was sad that Shepherd Alan was not with them. Jack and Dick told her not to fear. 'He is still under the mound; we shall bring him out at dusk.'

Joshua had crept to beneath the window and heard everything that was said. There were tales he had heard of fairy gold beneath the mounds, and he thought if he could discover the spell to open the mound he could have more treasure than any goodwife might bring him. So, he sneaked after the boys at dusk. Jack and Dick followed the distant music to the mound and danced around it three times, counting: 'Yan, tyan, tethera.' And after three circuits the mound opened, they heard the music more loudly, and out came Shepherd Alan. 'Now there are three of us,' they said, 'and we must hurry home, for the People of the Hill have other business now.'

Joshua thought he had seen how to open the mound, but he had not understood that three and seven are magical numbers which the hill must obey. He danced around the mound widdershins, counting as he went: 'Hant, tant, tothery, fothery, fant, sahny, dahny, downy, dominy, dik, haindik, taindik, totherydik.' And after thirteen circuits the mound opened to the sound of harsh music. As Joshua leapt greedily inside, the mound snapped shut behind him and he began to fall, yelling with fright, falling and yelling, falling and yelling. People who understand these things, like Jack and Dick, say he has been falling and yelling ever since, and will be falling and yelling until the end of time.

Jack and Dick brought Shepherd Alan home to great rejoicing, for he had been lost and now was found, and the seven of them – for within the year Goodwife Hannah gave birth to Mary – lived happily ever after.

SOURCE

Briggs, Katharine M., *A Dictionary of British Folk-Tales in the English Language*, 1971

Katharine Briggs tells us this story was collected by two Wiltshire folklorists from their grandmother, who had heard it from her Cumberland family nurse.

So, this may or may not be a Berkshire tale, though it is certainly a downland story, and as it is such a good folk tale and was not included in Kirsty Hartsiotis' highly recommended *Wiltshire Folk Tales*, it would be remiss of us not to include it here.

We have chosen Lambourn as the setting for the tale. Lambourn is a peaceful, pretty downland village in west Berkshire, the kind of place where Shepherd Alan and Goodwife Hannah might well have lived. It still has a church and an inn for you to visit.

SEVENTEEN

WANTAGE

Leaving The Lamb, we walked through the town to the church. St Michael and All Angels has stood here for nearly 1,000 years and its cruciform design has survived numerous improvements and restorations. Outside the churchyard is an ancient market cross; here the wagonette awaited our explorations and we mounted to resume our journey.

From Lambourn we went north across the Lambourn Downs, famed not only for sheep, as the name suggests, but also for horse training. Crossing the Ridgeway, a prehistoric route used long before the coming of the Romans, we edged gently down the steep hill on the other side. At the bottom of the hill we turned right and followed the curve of the ridge for a while before turning north through Letcombe Bassett and Letcombe Regis. An ancient camp, known locally as Letcombe Castle, stands on the Ridgeway above these villages, and an argument ensued between Mr Rowland and Dr Benjamin – Mr Rowland claiming the site was a Roman encampment and Dr Benjamin insisting that it was clearly an ancient British town. The area is certainly rich in history. Court Rolls for the manor of Letcombe Regis are amongst the oldest in the kingdom; these Rolls, and some of the wooden tallies used in the reign of Henry III early in the thirteenth century, are still in perfect preservation, and may be seen at the Public Record Office in London.

Discussions on Letcombe and its history lasted till we drove into Wantage. Mr Cleave informed us that there was a large brass and iron foundry here and that the manufacture of agricultural implements had increased as the making of hempen cloth declined. He particularly wanted to see the Wantage Tramway which connects the town to Wantage Road railway station, 2½ miles outside the town.

Wantage is a market town and is said to occupy the site of a Roman station. We had missed the market, which takes place on Wednesdays, and the July cherry fair was not till next week, so the marketplace was peaceful. A fine statue of King Alfred the Great stands at its centre, commemorating the monarch who was born in the town. Lunch awaited us at The Bell Inn, which overlooks the marketplace, and after lunch Professor Gaunt told us of Alfred's early years.

THE RAVEN OF EARTHLY TERROR (1) – BATTLE OF ASSEDONE

Christianity had come to the Kingdom of Wessex barely 100 years before Ælfred was born. It lay like a thin pall over the rich earth of earlier belief, the old religion which many still honoured. Ælfred was born in the village of Waneting, the youngest son of King Æthelwulf of Wessex and his first wife, Osburga. Osburga publicly supported her husband and sovereign in his advocacy of the Christian faith whilst privately practising the old religion.

Æthelwulf was tolerant of his wife's beliefs, even allowing her to call their son Ælfred, meaning Elf Counsel; Osburga believed elves were a race of divine beings endowed with magical powers, and she willed upon her baby son powers of insight and good counsel. And so it proved.

In time Osburga was to teach Ælfred her way of deep spiritual contemplation. But he was a sickly child and, fearing he might die, his father took him to Rome to be blessed by Pope Leo IV. Leo was much taken with the boy; he blessed him and prophetically anointed him as king in his father's presence, though his three elder brothers were in line before him. Father and son stayed in Rome for a year, and young though he was, Ælfred gained there an appreciation of Christian prayer and devotion. So it was that Ælfred's beliefs united the spiritual insights both of the Christian faith and of the old religion. And so, though he suffered a painful, recurring illness throughout his life, he was always strong in mind and spirit.

When his brother Æthelred became King of Wessex, after the short reigns of his elder brothers, Ælfred, at the age of eighteen, was declared his heir and second in command by the wise men of the Witan. A royal prince, and near as he now was to the throne of Wessex, Ælfred reflected on the prophetic words of Pope Leo IV. Within two years, Ælfred was fighting the invading Danes alongside his brother King Æthelred.

Having vanquished Norphymbre, East Anglia and the eastern part of Mercia with their Great Heathen Army, the Viking chiefs, Bacsecq and brothers Ivar the Boneless, Ubbe and Halfdan Ragnarsson, turned their eyes towards the Kingdom of Wessex. Ivar the Boneless was a cunning warrior chief and a clever tactician. Ubbe was a giant, 7ft tall and the cruellest man ever to tread upon English soil; after every victory, he slew all his Saxon adversaries, soldiers, priests, old men and children alike. Mothers throughout the land warned their children, 'Don't be naughty or Ubbe will get you.'

The Vikings sailed their longboats up the Temes, disembarking by the tiny hamlet of Elentone, and sent scouts ahead. When they reported the royal villa at Readingum to be poorly defended, the Danes, with Ubbe and Bacsecq at their head, moved swiftly to capture it and set about fortifying it as their base against Wessex.

To consolidate their gains, Ubbe sent a raiding party deeper into Wessex, but at Hingefelda they were ambushed by Æthelwulf, Ealdorman of Wessex. Æthelwulf was Wessex's most powerful warrior. He had a lean, powerful body with nerves and muscles of steel. Such was his charisma that his soldiers would follow him into the jaws of Hell. Æthelwulf and his forces drove the Viking raiders back to their Readingum base, where for the moment the Viking army was contained.

On the heels of this victory, King Æthelred decided on a direct attack upon Ubbe's Readingum base whilst fortification was still underway, with such forces as were immediately available to him. Alas, it was too late; the defences were already too strong for Æthelred's forces to break through and the attack was repulsed. Seeing Æthelred's small Saxon army retreating towards the downland to the west, Ubbe and Bacsecq led the bulk of the Great Heathen Army after them.

Meanwhile, Ælfred had been in deep reflection about the critical dangers facing the Kingdom of Wessex. When he emerged from his contemplative state, he immediately went to search where his white mare grazed. Ælfred's white mare, Epona, was an important symbol for him, representing the power of the horse goddess – which Wessex sorely needed as it faced the fight with the Viking army.

Ælfred leapt onto Epona and galloped her bare-backed to the top of Blowingstone Hill, where stood the ancient Blowing Stone with its deep holes and perforations. Ælfred knew the legend that anyone able to make the Blowing Stone sound a note would become king of all England. Upheld both by the power of the horse goddess and the prophecy of Pope Leo IV, he confidently blew the Blowing Stone. As a profound booming note echoed over the downs and far beyond, summoning the Wessex fyrd, men gathered their arms and left their farms, woods, smithies and workshops to gather on the Berkshire Downs, the 'Ash Down', to face a fierce and determined foe.

After their success at Readingum, Bacsecq, Ubbe and Ivar the Boneless felt confident of victory. They encamped in the hill fort at Offentona and assembled their mighty army on its western slope, taking the high ground. In the midst of the Viking ranks was held high their war banner, the Raven of Earthly Terror, symbol of Thor's might, woven by the Norns, three powerful maiden giantesses who spin the threads of men's fate. The Raven of Earthly Terror had already been witness to much fateful slaughter and the overthrow of many kingdoms in Thor's name.

The Wessex fyrd was gathered to a man, and King Æthelred's even mightier army was drawn up on the downland below. The two armies waited. Ubbe and Bacsecq were unwilling to relinquish the high ground and Æthelred was unwilling to assail it. The soldiers were close enough to shout insults and curses at each other, disparaging their foes' manhood and parentage.

Ælfred was keen to engage the enemy forthwith, but Æthelred chose to spend the lull before battle at a church nearby, praying for

a worthy outcome. Fretting for swift action, Ælfred's eye was caught by a thorn tree at the edge of the battleground, which calmed him and gave him pause for that deep thought which was always, for him, a source of insight and inspiration. For the old religion, the thorn was a sacred tree, a portent of challenges ahead and the promise of betterment once the challenges had been faced and overcome. For the Christian faith, the crown of thorns was a symbol of Christ's agony and his triumph over sin and death. And for Ælfred it was a sign of triumph over the Danes in the impending battle.

With these insights, Ælfred felt ready for battle. He surveyed the battle scene: the Danes were in an advantageous position on high ground, well disciplined, waiting patiently for their opponents to become disheartened before they struck; the Saxons were made edgy and impatient by the protracted lull and a king who had left the field. In the absence of his brother, Ælfred gave the order to attack.

With shields held high, spears held forward and loud shouts, the Wessex army moves swiftly up the slope, their shield wall well in place. The Viking army is caught on the hop by this sudden charge, its shield wall is not quite in place, and many in its front rank are speared before it recovers from the impact of the attack and reinforces its shield wall. But the confidence of the Viking hordes has been dented, the advantage of high ground has been lost, and the men of Wessex drive at them with increased vigour.

The Saxons stand shoulder to shoulder in the shield wall. Their wide, round shields are of lime wood, light and strong and hard to penetrate. Their bossed shields abut, so each man protects himself and the warrior to his left. The ranks behind stand ten deep, so when one man falls there is another to take his place, and another, and another... The shield wall is an organic engine of death fuelled by the bodies of men. To be in the shield wall is to know absolute horror and terror and utter despair of life and soul.

The battle is a clamorous clash of shield walls: the front rank slaying with swords; the second rank with spears; the ranks behind pushing and pushing, trying to force the opposing shield wall back, into disorder, to break and penetrate the wall. With the weight of numbers, about 1,000 more, Wessex prevails. Bacsecq and five of his earls have been slain. Thousands of corpses, Danes and Saxons, lie on the 'Ash Down'. Ashes to ashes. The Danes scatter. Ubbe flees north into Mercia, bearing with him the Raven of Earthly Terror. Ivar the Boneless flees south to Hungreford, where, ignominiously, he falls into a marsh and is drowned.

When the battle is over, Ælfred retrieves his white mare, Epona, where she grazes below Blowingstone Hill. With solemn countenance he canters to the thorn tree. There he dismounts, and, kneeling before the tree, he offers prayers for the souls of the slain, be they Saxon or Dane, to the Christ who wore the crown of thorns. Then, he leads Epona to the figure of the White Horse below the hill fort. Prostrating himself, he gives thanks to the horse goddess for giving him this victory over the Danes.

❧

Alas for Wessex, the Battle of Assedone proved to be a pyrrhic victory. Two weeks later the Danes defeated the Saxon army at

Basengum, and again at Mertone, where Æthelred was slain. Ælfred became King of Wessex and the prophecy of Leo IV was fulfilled.

SOURCES

Summers, Revd W.H. and Peake, Harold (Eds), *The Story of Hungerford in Berkshire*, 1926

Westwood, Jennifer and Simpson, Jacqueline, *The Lore of the Land*, 2006

Ekwall, Eilert, *Concise Oxford Dictionary of English Place-Names*, 1960

~

'The profoundest truth of war,' according to Liddell Hart, 'is that the issue of battles is usually decided in the minds of the opposing commanders, not in the bodies of their men.' This is surely true of Alfred.

When you stand on the western ramparts of Uffington Castle, you might reflect on the thousands of Saxons and Danes whose bodies once littered the Berkshire Downs below you.

You might find Bacsecq's burial mound, which folk say is somewhere on the Berkshire Downs. Various theories as to which are Bronze/Iron Age mounds and which are later, and whether the Danes buried their more important dead in existing mounds, have been hotly debated.

The Battle of Assedone took place on 8 January 871. The historical aspects of the story are generally accurate.

Eighteen

DRAGON HILL

We spent a little time exploring Wantage and then headed west past East Challow and the crossroads at Childrey, whose manor was occupied by Charles I on the night of 10 April 1644 on his march from Oxford to Marlborough. We stopped briefly at Sparsholt, the Revd Plumb having informed us that the church contained some ancient and interesting tombs and monuments. These included three effigies, all hollow and carved in wood: two ladies and a knight.

At last we came to the crossroads at Kingston Lisle, where we turned left and went a little way up the road to examine the aforementioned Blowing Stone. These days this huge sarsen stone, 3ft tall, is supported against a wide spreading tree at the front of a small tavern. On weekdays, the 'Lion', as it is known locally, is exhibited upon payment of a small fee. The landlord then unfastens the padlock and chain which secure the hinged wooden lid covering the mouthpiece. The exhibitor then blows into the aperture as into a horn, producing a loud low note that can, apparently, be heard by the Squire within Kingston Hall some three quarters of a mile away.

After the demonstration, all the gentlemen crossed the landlord's palm to try their skill. A delighted Mr Vanderpump was the only one to succeed, and was jokingly told that he must be a descendant of Alfred.

Returning to the crossroads, we turned west until we came to Dragon Hill. Here we alighted from the wagonette and climbed up the steep cart track and steeper hill, where Mr Rowland told us the story of a strange dragon.

KING GAARGE AND THE DRAGON

Everybody has a serpent inside, so they say, coiled at the base of the spine. I know it's true for me, because when I was six I woke one morning to find mine coiled on my pillow. It looked like a large earthworm, pinkish-purple in colour. It seemed quite friendly, for an earthworm, so we decided to keep it as a pet. That's my little sister Wynflaeth, which means beautiful and fair in our language (which she was), and me, Ethelinda, which means noble snake. My mother and father should never have called me that, as the tragedy which followed might never have happened.

We chopped up leftover vegetables to feed my worm, and it grew very quickly. It was 12in long in no time so we called it Draca, which means dragon in our language, because English dragons are really big worms, not like those Welsh dragons I've heard of with wings and fiery breath.

Draca had no eyes or ears so it couldn't see or hear us, yet it always sensed when someone was there. One day, Draca disappeared; there was just a round hole in the earth, which it must have made when it crawled off. Then it popped its head out of the soil and waved it about, like it was saying, 'Peepo!' It just liked to burrow in the soil to moisten its skin. We loved to watch the way it stretched and contracted its body to slither along, and we were amazed how quickly it could go.

We spent a lot of our spare time with Draca, Wynflaeth and me, when we weren't herding the sheep or milking the cows or harvesting the crops. He loved it when I tickled the top of his head; he waved his – it wasn't really a tail – bottom end with delight. When he became big enough, Draca let us ride on his back as he rushed across the fields. He seemed to enjoy it as much as Wynflaeth and me.

Then something terrible happened. The land for miles and miles around was ruled by a warrior chieftain called Uther Pendragon. When he died they decided to bury him near us, just below our hill fort, which had been one of his favourite places, apparently. They built a great big burial mound – rocks of chalk covered by a thin layer of earth – and buried Uther in the middle of it along with all the golden treasure he'd got as Pendragon. But that wasn't the terrible part.

The terrible part was what happened to Draca. It seemed like he could smell the golden treasure. When the warriors arrived with Uther's body and his treasure, Draca's head came up, pointing in their direction. He stayed like that, alert and motionless, for days. We knew he had no eyes or ears, and we thought he had no nose either, but he certainly had a nose for gold. He knew better than to go anywhere near the armed warriors as they dug the mound, but as soon as they were gone he was off, slithering across the landscape, his body moving like waves on a duck pond, until he reached the mound. Draca just left us and took possession of the mound and its buried gold.

Draca jealously guarded the mound and its gold. It was his gold now and he allowed nobody near it. If anybody went near the mound (and some brave souls tried at first), he would lash them with his bottom end and they would scurry away with bruised behinds. Nobody could get near, not even Wynflaeth, no one but me; after all, he was my worm, or maybe I was his. He still enjoyed me tickling his head, always did, right to the end.

It seemed like he somehow took energy from the gold which made him ravenously hungry. He took small creatures at first; mice and rats and hare living around the foot of the mound. He had a way of opening his mouth very wide and taking a creature whole, then sucking it down into his crop so he could digest it slowly. That was when his breath began to smell, with all that rotting flesh in his crop.

As he grew larger and larger he foraged further afield. That was when he started on our sheep. He would slither up to a grazing sheep and, before it knew what was happening, Draca had opened his great maw and it was gone in a single gulp, sucked down into his crop. That was when we noticed that he only took sheep, even ones with long horns, never rams – his taste was for females of any species he fancied.

The most terrible day was when he took Wynflaeth. She was sitting on her little three-legged stool under the cow's udder, grinning fondly at me and contentedly milking the cow into a big wooden pail. When Draca slid up she didn't take much notice as she was used to him being around. Only when he opened his great maw did she look alarmed – it happened so fast – one slurp and she disappeared.

I rushed at him, beating him with a stick, but it was hopeless; she was already in his crop. One moment she was there, so beautiful and fair a maiden, the next she was gone. Then Draca slurped the milk from the pail, slid under the cow's udder, and sucked her dry. I was so full of sadness and tears over losing my lovely Wynflaeth, and so cross with Draca, that I wouldn't tickle his head for weeks.

After that he had a taste for milk and maidens, and would take no other. No maiden was safe from him; he could muscle his way across fields faster than any maid could run. Cows had no chance. Some maidens gave up being maidens to avoid becoming Draca's dinner, but it turned out he was not that choosy.

Draca grew enormous on his diet of milk and maidens. I mean really, really big. If you go there now you can still see the deeply scored landscape where his great bulk slimed across it. When he wasn't foraging for his dinner he lay coiled around what we came to call Draca's Dun, which means Dragon's Hill in our language, his vast tube of a body seemingly drawing energy from his precious gold. And with all those rotting maidens and sour milk in his crop, the stench of his breath was disgusting, and what with his bad behaviour as well, he was known far and wide as the Loathly Worm.

The men decided something had to be done. Their solution was to draw lots every day to see which maiden was to be given to Draca for his dinner, along with six pails of milk. This put control back in our hands, they said. Typical! It was actually my father's idea – did I mention he was the local chief in charge of the hill fort?

So, every day a maiden was chosen by lot, her hands and feet were tied, and she was left with six pails of milk close to Draca's Dun (but not too close, on account of his abominable breath). One day it was my turn. It had to come, even if I was the chief's daughter. Only the day before I'd been on the mound tickling his head. I'd had to forgive him for gobbling up Wynflaeth – it was just his nature after all. Now, there I was trussed up with six pails of milk and left there for his dinner.

Then it all happened at once. As soon as he saw who'd been left for his dinner he began to howl. He'd never howled before – I didn't even know he *could* howl. He howled like he was suffering a terrible anguish; well, I could see he was, howling and casting his great head from side to side. I could see he had a whole lot on his mind, wondering what to do, him being my worm and all. He was still howling when King Gaarge turned up, cantering slowly out the misty west, as my mother said (she always gave herself airs, being a chief's woman).

He cantered up to me, got down from his horse (bit of an old nag, I thought) and told me to call him King Gaarge. 'Call me King Gaarge,' he said, 'scourge of dragon-kind. The dread news of your Loathly Worm has passed from mouth to mouth over hill and vale to my abode far in the west. Now I am here there is no more cause to fear.' He'd get on well with my mother, I thought.

He looked about as much of a scourge as a stick of celery, but he did have this big sword which he liked to brandish as he strode about, going on and on about all the dragons he had slain, while I lay there trussed, with Draca howling and his noxious breath making the milk curdle.

Finally, thank the goddess, he marched off up the mound, waving his sword. He had some pluck, I'll say that for him, clambering over the clammy coils. He'd never have got away with it if Draca had been himself – he'd have swallowed him whole, and belched him back out probably, sword and all. But, poor Draca, he was in such torment over being given his own as his dinner that he didn't see what was coming. With five swift strokes King Gaarge plunged his sword into each of Draca's five hearts and it was all over for Draca. No contest.

Afterwards, King Gaarge boasted about his great victory over the Loathly Worm to anybody who wanted to listen, which was everybody except me. Only I knew about Draca's inglorious end, and nobody was interested in my story: it wasn't racy enough.

King Gaarge really got under my skin. He was so pompous, so conceited, as he told them how he had leapt in to save the maiden, the chief's daughter even, as the dragon was about to devour her;

how he had withstood the dragon's fiery breath – I couldn't see a
scorch mark on him – wielding his mighty sword, receiving many
ferocious blows from the dragon's tail – I couldn't see a bruise
on him – how despite being a puny human against such a mighty
foe – I agreed with him there – his experience as the scourge of
dragon-kind had prevailed and he had struck the blow which
brought the dread beast its demise. He even had the cheek to
say that the dragon's venomous blood had seared the ground on
the mound's summit so nothing would grow there ever after –
I knew it was just chalk showing through the thin soil.

So, that was the story which has been told ever since, King Gaarge and the Dragon on Dragon Hill – and, I can tell you, it's pure myth. I hope, after listening to my story, you'll credit what really happened; after all, I was there, the worm was mine, and I was his.

SOURCES

Newbury and District Field Club, 1912

Simpson, Jacqueline and Roud, Steve, *A Dictionary of English Folklore*, 2000

Vinycomb, John, *Fictitious and Symbolic Creatures in Art*, 1906

When you stand on Dragon Hill, beneath Uffington Castle and the White Horse, gaze at the surrounding landscape; you can believe the dragon's great bulk scored those deep channels in the earth.

This tale blends together two folk myths: (1) King Gaarge killed the dragon on Dragon Hill, and where its blood was spilt nothing will ever grow; (2) Dragon Hill is the burial mound of Uther Pendragon. Then another English dragon is added to the mix: 'The Laidly Worm of Spindleston Heugh.'

UFFINGTON

Rested after the story, we decided to climb the hillside on the opposite side of the track to view the famous White Horse, which gives the vale its name. Up close, this is a curious hill figure and Mr Cleave said it didn't look much like a horse to him: 'What kind of a horse has a beak?'

As we walked up the hillside to Uffington Castle, Dr Benjamin informed us that this hill fort was smaller than the one at Letcombe Regis, thus re-energising the debate over the age of the Letcombe site. A local shepherd in the vicinity was called on to give his opinion. He had no view as to the age of the site, but said the Revels held here were not to be missed. He also told us that the White Horse could be seen more clearly from Uffington, so we postponed our visit to Wayland's Smithy and descended into the vale. We were directed to a spot to the west of the village which gave a long view, and it was indeed more horse-like from a distance.

A description of the village is given in the opening chapter of *Tom Brown's Schooldays*, and we recognised the tiny schoolroom by the church, where Tom is first taught before being sent away to Rugby. Revd Plumb pointed out the unusual octagonal tower that rises from the centre of the ancient cruciform church. The churchyard contains some fine yew trees and within the church are several interesting tombs and memorials.

We had been informed that the landlord of the White Horse Inn was a splendid and genial host, but unfortunately this hostelry was closed for some reason so we continued on to the Fox and

Hounds in the High Street. Here we stopped for the night, and after dinner the landlord introduced us to a shepherd, who told us tales of White Horse Revels in years gone by.

WHITE HORSE REVELS

Storyteller

I once met an owd Vale shepherd, Jethro Aldridge were 'is name, grazed 'is sheep o' the hill all around t' White 'orse. He had a weather-beaten face, a quick smile, and long hair bleached white i' t' summer sun. He told me all about t' Scouring o' the White 'orse and t' Revels which followed. This is Jethro's tale, just as he told it t' me; well, more or less:

Scouring the White Horse

'Twere every seventh year we Scoured the White 'orse, cleared away all the grass and weeds what had encroached upon it for seven years past. Our family, we allas scoured the eye – 'twere a great honour – allas had done for thousands o' years, ever since we first cut the White 'orse out o' the turf.

My, what Revels we had then; it's all come down the family, told and retold till it's like we were there. At Midsummer Solstice

we had this great fire festival, you know, to honour Father Sun. Built great fires we did, and called on Father Sun to give summer a good boost while we gathered in our winter provisions. The young lads made great sun circles out of hay held together with tar. They set them alight and rolled them down the steepest part o' the hill, what we call the Manger these days, and ran after them shouting and laughing and rolling down themselves. While we had the fires going, we took the chance to fumigate the cattle to get rid of ringworm and scabs and warts.

The Revels

O'course, we have Revels still, but now they've moved from Midsummer Solstice to just after Autumn Equinox, at Michaelmas. Mm! Our old priest reckons Michaelmas is about St Michael and the other archangels casting out Lucifer, which he says is Latin and means light-bearer. Funny that, casting out the light this time o' year.

Last time we Scoured the White 'orse, near on 15,000 folk turned up for the Revels, all in their Sunday best, the toffs in velvet coats, the farmers in fustian, and the yokels in clean smocks. It was one o' those warm, bright early autumn days, like Father Sun giving summer a final boost. Me and my wife Alice and our two big lads Alfred and Arthur were there. Those two fancied their chance at the sports; they'd been practising all summer. Alfred was tough and strong and liked to wrestle, Arthur was more wiry and agile and liked Berkshire backsword fighting; both of them were keen to have a go at the greasy pole.

On the sloping ground to the east of Uffington Castle they'd set up a fair. It had booths and stalls, all decorated with brightly coloured flags and flowers, selling nuts, apples, gingerbread, toys, ribbons, knives, braces, straps, oh all sorts o' stuff. There were musicians, acrobats, jugglers, fire-eaters. A publican from Abingdon had a booth selling ale and stout and cider, with a skittle alley beside it.

The Master of Ceremonies for the sports was a farmer, Eli Edginton, known for his very loud voice: 'The sports will kick off with a foot race up the side of the hill. Hurry up to the starting line.' Thirteen big lads went running and jostling one another, while a little lad nipped round them and won the race; the big lads were right put out.

'Roll up, roll up for the next event,' bellowed Eli. 'This is a race down the steep face of the hill into the Manger chasing a painted cartwheel. The prize for the winner is a whole wheel of our good Vale cheese.'

I suppose this was a hangover from our old fire festivals. The cartwheel was set rolling and the men had to chase after it. There were a lot o' terrible falls, some o' the men rolling more than 50 yards, while others somersaulted down the hill after the cartwheel. At one time they'd have raced skidding down on 'orses' jawbones, but they don't do that no more.

After sack racing for children, Eli announced with a chortle, 'Now for something really special: sack racing for the ladies. Wait for it, wait for it, and the prize is, the prize is,' he paused, 'the finest Holland Unmentionables!' he yelled. 'Yes ladies, you could be the proud wearer of Holland Unmentionables, so don't rush all at once, line up, line up.'

I dug Alice in the ribs, 'Go on Alice, it'll be a laugh.'

She gave me her most withering look. 'What, show the hoi polloi my bloomers, even if I hadn't worn 'em yet? Laugh is it? I'd be the laughing stock o' the Vale.'

All the other women must have thought the same so the race was called off. Pity, I'd have liked her in Holland Unmentionables.

Eli was disappointed as well. 'Well, well, if we can't have Holland Unmentionables we'll have a bit of jingling instead.'

The man who was 'it' was stripped to the waist and a bell was tied round him. Then he was chased by a dozen blindfolded men running after the bell, all bumping into one another and falling about. The one as caught him was 'it' next, until one strapping lad evaded capture for fifteen minutes and won the prize. It was a great laugh, the crowd all shouting and guffawing, but I couldn't take my mind off Holland Unmentionables.

Any road, the greasy pole distracted me. It had a leg o' mutton at the top, fair near 15ft off the ground, the prize for the first to reach it. Alfred and Arthur were keen to have a go, first in the queue they were – they reckoned that gave them the best chance. I was swapping yarns about shepherding with little old Horace Jarvis from over Lambourn way. He had a great grin on his face watching all the likely lads sliding down the pole one after another. 'Just wait and see,' he said with a chuckle, 'it's me what'll walk home with the mutton. When these young lads have wiped all the grease off on their breeches, I'll shin up in no time.' He was right too.

Eli announced the race I was most eager to watch: 'Them taking part in the next race line up at the top of the hill next to the cart. This is the most dangerous race of the day, chasing a Berkshire pig down the hill. Whoever runs down and seizes the pig gets to keep it.'

The pig was a massive, tawny red, bony beast, spotted with black. Its body was long and thick, with short powerful legs. Its pendulous ears pricked forward. It was grunting and snorting with rage and kicking the sides o' the cart.

As soon as it's released, this great gallant grunter starts from the cart with surprising speed, eighteen men in pell-mell pursuit, amid the cheers of thousands. Some pursuers fall head over heels down the steep slope and out o' the race. By the time the hog hits open country, the only ones left in the running are Walter Rutter, Billy Bushnell, and Abner Bailey, all of them old hands who have caught the pig in the past. They run neck and neck for half a mile before Walter begins to falter and puffing Billy runs out o' steam.

With a sudden change of speed, light-footed Abner is only 2 yards behind the hog, letting the pig set the pace. It's a trial of endurance now. They run another half mile. Abner has settled into a rhythm, making long strides. The pig's little legs are a blur of movement, its great pot-belly swinging from side to side. It seems to be tiring, until, with a lightning turn, it faces its pursuer: its mouth agape; its bulk bearing down on slender Abner; its razor-sharp tusk teeth striking at Abner's throat.

Abner remains so still that everything seems to happen in slow motion. In its flying leap towards Abner's throat, the pig's feet are off the ground.

Abner waits calmly, somehow now with a loop o' binding twine between his fingers. Slowly swaying sideways, Abner slips the loop unerringly around the pig's forelegs, letting its momentum tighten the twine while it's still in the air. The pig hits the ground hard then overbalances onto its fat side. Abner swiftly knots the binding twine and ties up the pig's hind legs as well before it can recover. The hog is his. The young men who chased after the runners carry Abner back shoulder-high, and the vast crowd shout and cheer the victor for a good fifteen minutes.

☙

Then it was the time Alfred and Arthur had been waiting for. A ring had been set up in Uffington Castle for prize fighting, wrestling and backsword fencing. A great crowd filled the wide space inside the castle or sat on the surrounding banks for a good view. I'd gone in early with my lads and was up at the edge o' the ring, where I first noticed the London lads, from down the Mile End Road somebody reckoned. Big beggars they were, tough-looking too.

'Gather round, gather round,' Eli called out. 'First in the ring we have the prize fighting contest.' This was vicious bare-knuckle fighting, leaving a lot of battered faces and sore kidneys. Then, 'The final bout in this contest is between Oscar Cufflin from Stepney, 6ft 6in tall and weighing in at fifteen stone, who has got through to the final without a scratch, and our own Ezra Baskerville from Blewbury, all of 4ft 2in and weighing in at nine stone. A right David and Goliath match if ever there was one.'

The bout lasted forty-five minutes, a trial of brawn against guile. A single hit from Oscar's gargantuan hams would have broken Ezra in two, but with his constantly dancing feet he took only glancing blows, heavy though they were. But he was hardy, and handy with it, getting in some telling blows to Oscar's flanks and kidneys, wearing him down.

After forty-five minutes, Ezra was still dancing but Oscar was tiring and letting down his guard. Ezra dodged a wild right hook from Oscar's flailing fists and then, leaping up, delivered a stinging bare-knuckle blow behind Oscar's left ear. As Oscar reeled, Ezra's hard knuckles delivered four more fast blows between his eyes

☙

– left right left right – as final as the stone what did for Goliath, and, like Goliath, Oscar keeled over and hit the ground like a falling tree. Ezra walked away with the crown of bay leaves, a fifty guinea purse, and a sheepish smile for the cheering crowd.

Then Eli announced the wrestling contest: one fall or one submission to win each bout. Alfred was confident, having almost reached the final seven years before, but I knew he had tough opposition from the London lad who Eli introduced as 'That famous fighter, the Merciless Mile End Monster, Mickie Maddox'. He looked like a monster too. His wide face in a huge head was covered in blackened scars, his nose was squashed into his face, his ears looked like they'd been half chewed, he wore black breeches, he had black hair close-cropped and matted black hair all over his bulging bare arms and torso.

Mickie Maddox won bout after bout, by fair means or, more usually, foul. Great powerful men who had carried off many prizes in the county were tossed about the ring. In his first bout he lifted his opponent at full stretch and threw him right out o' the ring, to the delight o' the crowd. His second opponent he stabbed with a series of fierce forearm jabs till he fell fainting to the floor. His third opponent, a bulky experienced wrestler, put up more of a fight, till Maddox kicked his legs from under him with such force that he was unable to get up. He never fully recovered afterwards.

Between his own bouts, Alfred watched Maddox carefully, thinking he might have the measure of him. When they met in the final, Alfred twisted away whenever Maddox tried to get him in an arm lock and lift him from the ground to throw him around the ring; and he skipped away from Maddox's vicious kicks to his legs.

Finally, Alfred caught Maddox in a body lock and was lifting him from the ground when Maddox leaned back, grabbed Alfred by the ears, pulled him through the air and caught him in a headlock, his hands locked tightly together for leverage. It turned out later that the headlock was Maddox's speciality. He practised on a wooden head in two parts with strong springs between – never went anywhere without it – so he had the strength to put pressure on his opponent's jugular. Starved of blood to the brain, Alfred submitted just before passing out.

Eli's stentorian tones resounded about the castle: 'The final contest is with our own cudgel of choice, the Berkshire backsword.'

Arthur was good at backsword fencing; he won each bout with ease until he reached the final and had to face Simon Stone, from South Marston over the border in Wiltshire, a veteran backsword fighter.

They were cunning, accomplished and well-matched swordsmen, carefully circling each other, attempting a strike at their opponent's head, always parried, neither gaining an advantage. Suddenly, the tempo of the fight increased, blow upon blow, the crack o' the ash sticks echoing around the field – crack crack crack crack – now high to the head, now low to the legs, until Arthur got in a lucky blow to Simon's temple, harder than intended, for the aim is not to maim. Simon swooned to the ground, and it was some minutes before he regained consciousness and Arthur felt able to claim his prize. He was never to do so.

There was a change of tone in the surrounding throng, a sudden hush, which made Arthur turn to see what was happening. The crowd parted to allow a young man in an immaculate black velvet coat and breeches and tricorn hat, a broad smile on his handsome face, to enter the ring. It was Arthur's boyhood friend Tim Gibbons, an Uffington man turned highwayman on the Great West Road. He had tied his black 'orse to an ancient thorn tree and walked up the hill to challenge the winner to a duel, their fifty guinea prize against his black stallion.

Before Arthur gathered his wits to respond, Eli was quick to leap in, 'And now, ladies and gentlemen, you are going to see a surprise contest between the two best backswordsmen in the county, Arthur Aldridge and the infamous Tim Gibbons, gentleman of the road, fighting for the fifty guinea purse against a fine black stallion.'

O'course, it was hardly a fair contest, as that rogue Tim Gibbons well knew – and Eli, come to that – with Arthur, weary after several bouts and a tough one with Simon Stone and not expecting another fight, and Tim fresh on the field.

Arthur fought manfully, as I would expect of him, but it was soon clear how much greater was Tim's energy and speed, and after receiving several blows to the body Arthur ruefully yielded the contest to save himself from serious injury. The two old friends embraced before Tim galloped off on his black stallion to avoid arrest, better off by fifty guineas.

So, my sturdy sons came away from the White 'orse Revels empty-handed, as did my wife Alice, and I was left with these memories of all that had occurred and thoughts o' Holland Unmentionables. Oh yes, and I suppose you want to know what contest I put myself in for. Well, it was the pipe-smoking marathon, from which I came away – contented.

SOURCES

Newbury and District Field Club, 1912
Ditchfield, P.H. (Ed.), *Bygone Berkshire*, 1975
Hammond, Nigel, *Rural Life in the Vale of the White Horse 1780-1914*, 1997

These various sources describe the rich and colourful folk tales of the Scouring of the White Horse and the accompanying Revels which are brought together in this story.

Scouring the White Horse is now carried out periodically by the National Trust, who are the custodians of the site. You can volunteer to take part in Scouring the White Horse.

TWENTY

WAYLAND'S SMITHY

The following morning, we again left the wagonette at the foot of the ridge, a little further west than the day before, and climbed up Woolstone Hill to the Ridgeway. We walked west along this prehistoric track till we came to the grove of beech trees that surrounds the Neolithic long barrow known as Wayland's Smithy. Last night the locals in Uffington told us that Wayland, Norse god of metal working, had made his home here to be farrier to the White Horse and her foal, which has now disappeared. They also suggested that if a horse lost a shoe the owner could take it here and leave it with a sixpence. When the owner returned, the sixpence would be gone and the horse would be shod. Mr Cleave said anyone so foolish as to believe that would probably lose the horse as well as the sixpence.

The remains at 'Wayland's Cave' are described by William Camden in his *Britannia*, and Sir Walter Scott immortalised the area in his novel *Kenilworth*, so it is much visited in the summer months. The barrow is a remarkable construction of large, rough-hewn sarsen stones in front of a long earth mound that could have covered a dozen fallen heroes. Some scholars believed this to be the burial place of Bacsecq, a Danish general slain at Ashdown in 871. It appears there were once four altar cairns in front of the barrow, and you can imagine the people standing beyond the priestly enclosure whilst sacrifices were offered to their Scandinavian gods.

As we walked along the Ridgeway, I told a story. Wayland had an apprentice called Flibbertigibbet, whom he sent down

the Ridgeway to buy nails. On his way back, Flibbertigibbet
went on a hunt for birds' eggs, and was so absorbed that he
lost track of time and arrived back hours later than Wayland
expected. The enraged Wayland picked up one of the giant
sarsen stones and flung it at Flibbertigibbet, pinning him to
the ground by his heel. Flibbertigibbet sat snivelling by the
stone, and this area of the burial chamber has been known as
Snivelling Corner ever since.

My brother said the latest theory was that Wayland's Smithy
was already old when the Danes invaded, as his story of Wayland
would show:

Wayland the Smith

The warrior Wade was proud of his name. His family claimed
descent from the fabled God-Giant Wade, King of the Finns, father
of Wayland the Smith. His dream was to have three mighty sons
called Egil, Slagfid, and Wayland, like the God-Giant Wade himself. Already he had two sturdy sons, Egil and Slagfid, but Slagfid's
birth had been a difficult one, and no Wayland ever emerged.

Egil and Slagfid, imbued with tales of Wayland from the cradle,
felt they knew their imaginary friend and brother Wayland as well
as they knew each other. As they grew to be strong warriors they
always held Wayland and his stories in their hearts.

As the first fleet of Viking ships harried the shores of
Norphymbre, Egil and Slagfid were at the fore. What began as
a raid for women from the villages, and gold from the monastic
houses, grew into a colonial war with a raid on East Anglia. From
this base, under the command of brothers Halfdan Ragnarsson
and Ivar the Boneless, brothers Egil and Slagfid, now veterans of
warfare, fought their way with the conquering army into the rich
Saxon city of Eoforwic, which was taken and renamed Yorvik.
Norphymbre was conquered, Snotengaham was taken, Ivar the
Boneless subdued East Anglia, Mercia was brought to heel, and the
Danelaw was established throughout most of England.

Wessex was to be their next prize. With a fair wind, the Vikings
sailed their broad-bellied, 90ft longboats from East Anglia up the

Temes towards Wessex, disembarking opposite the cliffs below Taeppa's Tump, the Saxon warrior chieftain's burial mound.

Egil and Slagfid were sent deeper into Wessex, leading a raiding party to spy out the land. They took the Temes path further up the river, and then followed the ancient Ridgeway, where they found a long burial mound surmounted by ancient beech trees. Beneath the mound they pulled down a portal stone to reveal a narrow chamber. It was an ideal hideout for their party. In the gathering dusk they made camp within the chamber and drew close to their small fire.

As they had done many times before during martial campaigns, the warriors turned to Egil and Slagfid to tell their tale of Wayland the Smith. This was their story:

⁊

Three swan maidens, Olrun Wise Counsellor, Swanwhite Wise in Lore and Allwise the Fair, flew out of Murkwood to seek flax by the shore of Lake Wolfsiar in the forest of Wolfdales. They put off their swan forms before collecting a goodly supply of flax which they began to spin, telling tales, singing songs and laughing together as they worked.

In the forest of Wolfdales dwelt Egil and Slagfid and their younger brother Wayland. When he was but a boy, Wayland's father Wade had sent him as an apprentice to the elves of the Icelandic mountains, the finest workers in metal the world had ever known, yet Wayland soon outshone his teachers. At the end of his apprenticeship, Wayland had come to live with his brothers in Wolfdales, in the great gabled hall which they had built, to practise there his trade as a smith.

Often, the three brothers went into the forest to stalk deer or boar or bear. Returning with their winnings one day, the rare sound of women's voices caressed their ears, drawing them to the lake shore. Stalking their fresh game on soft feet, the sight of three beautiful, naked swan maidens spinning flax by the lake gladdened their hearts and stirred their loins. Creeping closer still, the brothers came upon the maidens' swan forms lying by the lake shore. These they seized and hid in a hollow tree. Then they quietly withdrew, to gaze upon the swan maidens from a distance.

⁊

Their work finished, the swan maidens strolled along the shore to retrieve their swan forms. But the swan forms were gone. As they cast around in consternation, Egil, Slagfid and Wayland came out from their hiding place.

'We live a lonely life in this forest,' said Egil bluntly. 'We have appealed to Odin for wives, and now here you are.'

The swan maidens grasped at once that their swan forms had been hidden. They willingly accepted their fate, to remain in Wolfdales as the wives of men. Olrun took Egil as her lover. Swanwhite took Slagfid. Allwise threw wanton arms round Wayland's white neck. As her golden hair brushed his cheeks, he became enchanted with her.

And so they lived a simple, contented life together in the great forest. Olrun, Swanwhite and Allwise collected the fruits of the forest: nuts, roots and berries. Egil and Slagfid hunted the rich game: deer, boar and bear. Wayland practised the art of a smith.

Wayland searched out where precious metals and stones were to be found and dug them out of the earth. He found iron and copper, silver and gold. He found gemstones of amber; to his delight, when he held these bright stones to the light, it seemed they had captured the warmth of the sun. And more than the sun, for within the gemstones he saw seeds and twigs; he saw where spiders crawled and bees spread their wings.

From these gifts of the earth, Wayland the Smith forged the accoutrements of the warrior and the finest of jewellery. He made helms and arm rings and breastplates of gold, and for himself he forged a mighty sword imbued with all his elven strength and skill.

He hammered out Thor's hammers to make talisman pendants. He twisted gold strands to form torcs and bracelets. He cast exquisite amulets to the pattern of forest flowers and trees, and wolves, deer, dragons and serpents. Everything he made was finely inlaid with his precious amber gems.

Oftentimes, when the wives were foraging and his brothers were hunting in the forest, Wayland took out Allwise's swan form and studied it with the practised eye of a highly skilled artisan. First he compared the swan's wing bones with his own arm. He saw how the swan's wing had an upper segment like his upper arm, attached to the breast bone via the shoulder blade and supported by powerful muscles between upper segment and breast. He saw how the upper segment attached to a middle segment, two bones like those in his forearm. He saw how wrist and hand were fused and lengthened to form the swan's third and lower segment.

Wayland carefully traced the wing feathers: tertials inlaid in the upper segment, secondaries inlaid in the larger bone of the middle segment, primaries inlaid in the lower segment, and coverts over all the quill-bases above and below.

He observed how the strength of muscles and articulation of joints between breast and shoulder blade, and the three wing segments, allowed for flapping, circling, gliding and folding.

He became so totally absorbed in the wing's anatomy that one day Allwise and her sisters, returning early from foraging, saw where the swan forms were hidden. For seven winters and more they had willingly dwelt with Egil, Slagfid and Wayland, knowing this to be their fate. Yet, more and more they longed to know again the exhilaration of flight and to return to their home in Murkwood. Now, their fate had turned.

Soon after, Egil, Slagfid and Wayland, returning from hunting with a fat boar and two deer, found the hall silent. The swan maidens had flown. In search of their wives, Egil strode east after Olrun, and Slagfid strode south after Swanwhite. Wayland remained in Wolfdales, hopefully and faithfully awaiting the return of his beloved, fair-haired Allwise, and spending his days at the forge.

He made many arm rings of red-gold enriched with precious gems, which he strung upon ropes of flax. Seven hundred he made.

Nidud, King of the Njars, hearing of Wayland working in Wolfdales alone, sent his warriors forth, their shield bosses white in the waning moon, their coats of mail glittering. They found the 700 arm rings in Wayland's hall, and unthreading them, they took only the finest. This was a ring of pure gold, inlaid with Wayland's most precious bees in amber, which was to have been his home-coming gift to Allwise the Fair.

Wayland returned from the hunt with a brown bear about his shoulders. He piled wind-dried logs and made a fierce fire to roast the bear, and then lay on a bearskin, counting his rings. The most exquisite, Allwise's homecoming gift, was gone. His heart rose in his breast; long he lay in rapture with the thought that Allwise had returned to his hearth, and he fell asleep with joy – only to wake with despair, fast-bound by fetters about his feet and chains about his hands.

'Who are the men who have chained and fettered me as I slept?' he cried.

Stepping forward, Nidud answered question with sneering question, 'What good have you got, greatest of elf smiths, from plundering my forest of Wolfdales of its treasure?'

Wayland replied, 'A greater treasure we enjoyed in former times in this happy hall and home, together with Olrun Wise Counsellor, Swanwhite Wise in Lore and Allwise the Fair.'

Nidud placed Allwise's homecoming ring on his daughter Bodvild's arm, and girded on Wayland's elven sword. Wayland, eyes grim as a serpent's, could only gnash his teeth in fury. Watching him with cruel pleasure, Nidud's wily wife pronounced Wayland's fate: 'Woeful shall he be who comes from the wood of Wolfdales.'

With brutal, sadistic relish, Nidud cut the ligaments in Wayland's knees, imprisoning him in his body, and then confined him to the island of Saeverstod. In return for meat, Wayland was made to fashion marvellous artefacts for the King alone.

In bitter anguish of heart, Wayland bemoaned his fate, 'From Nidud's hip there hangs the sword I tempered with a true hand

and sharpened with a sure eye. Now, the shining blade is stolen from me. Bitterest to bear, bitterest to behold, is Allwise's ring on Bodvild's arm.' Then, iron entered his heart and he made an oath, 'My elven blade shall yet be reforged and I shall be avenged.'

Soon after, the sons of Nidud sailed secretly to Saeverstod, with evil in their hearts, greedy to lay their hands on Wayland's store of metals and gems, which he kept in an iron box by his forge. Coming to Wayland's door with swaggering arrogance, they demanded of him the key to the box.

'Come tomorrow,' smiled Wayland. 'Come alone; tell neither maidens nor courtiers, let no one know of our meeting, and you shall receive your due.'

The brothers returned on the morrow, eagerly demanding the key to Wayland's treasure chest. They opened the chest in a shaft of sunlight. The shining gold and silver and precious gems brightened their eyes with greedy desire as the shaft of Wayland's reforged sword sliced the air and sliced their heads from their shoulders in a single stroke.

Wayland scraped hair and flesh from the skulls of Nidud's sons, and from the skulls he fashioned drinking cups set in silver as fitting gifts for Nidud and his wily wife. To bring Bodvild joy, he forged a brooch from her brothers' teeth. For Nidud's wife he crafted a thick gold torc, which he inlaid, at the very limit of his art, with the bright eyes of her sons. Nidud, his wife and his daughter received these gifts with smug pleasure at being the possessors of such treasures beyond price.

Equally beyond price to Bodvild was the arm ring which Nidud had given to her. Alas, she had broken it, and brought it to Wayland to repair without her father knowing, else she might incur his quick wrath.

'I can mend it so delicately,' said Wayland, 'that the ring shall appear to your father to be finer than before.' Wayland brought ale and invited Bodvild to sit with him, and they talked together. Bodvild listened as Wayland told her about the life he had enjoyed in Wolfdales, so different from the life endured at Nidud's harsh court. As Wayland talked, Bodvild began to see him as a man and to admire his gentleness and strength, and when he spoke of his longing for the return of Allwise she felt compassion for him. They lay together.

Wayland had gradually gathered swans' feathers from their colony on Saeverstod: primaries, secondaries, tertials and coverts. Now, he combined all he had learned about Allwise's wings, and the way he had worked the flesh of Nidud's sons, with the full extent of his skill as an elven smith. He devised an extension of forged and beaten silver to each hand, strong and light, to support the primaries. He cunningly and painfully remodelled his forearms and upper arms to implant secondaries and tertials, and fitted coverts over all the quill-bases.

Over the years Wayland had compensated for his withered legs by building yet more powerful muscles in his chest and arms. Now, he would teach himself to fly like a swan and escape his body's imprisonment.

The wife of Nidud, the wily one, came in where the lord of the Njars rested. 'Awake! Awake! Little sleep have I had since our sons are gone. I am cold with fear. I would speak with Wayland.'

Wayland was summoned. She asked him, 'Tell me Wayland, lord of the elves, where are my boys? What has befallen them?'

Wayland replied in thunderous tones, 'First you shall swear on oath – by ship's keel, by shield's rim, by stallion's shoulder, by steel's edge – that no harm shall come to the wife of Wayland, nor cause the death of his dear bride, who shall bring up our child in this hall.'

Confused, trembling with fear for her sons, and thinking he spoke of Allwise, she made the oath.

Wayland spoke to Nidud, King of the Njars, and his wily wife. His voice was stern and grim. 'I struck off the heads of your stalwart boys. Beneath soot-blackened, blood-spattered bellows their bodies are hid. I set their skulls in silver, from which you quaff your ale.'

Nidud's wife gasped in grief and horror, her hands flying to her cheeks and neck. Wayland went on, 'Your sons' bright eyes gaze sightless from the torc you touch about your neck. To bring Bodvild joy, I forged a brooch from her brothers' teeth. And yet more joy, for your dear daughter is now great with child.'

Wayland unfolded his wings. With bold beats of those white wings he, laughing, lifted out of reach of any sharp-eyed archer's arrow, calling as he rose, 'Woeful are they who brought me from the wood of Wolfdales.'

In bitter pain and sorrow, Nidud felt the fall of his house, knowing his longed-for vengeance was in vain.

Bodvild was brought forth and Nidud, in his agony, asked, 'Can it be true, as I hear, that on a day of ill omen you visited Wayland's isle and lay with him?'

Bodvild the bright-eyed maiden answered boldly, 'It is true, Nidud, as you were told, on the lone island we lay together. Against his wiles I had no wit to struggle. Against his will I had no wish to struggle.'

Wayland soared on strong wings over trees and hills to find a place where he might wait the return of his wife, Allwise the Fair, wherever and whenever this might be.

And so, the blood of he who sprang from Bodvild's womb has flowed through countless generations into the veins of those who have told this tale tonight.

❧

As the story ended, stillness came over the fighting men. Just beyond the circle of their fire-soft faces, they felt the rustle of bright wings and the deep, patient presence in this place of Wayland the Smith, awaiting the return of his love.

Later, Egil and Slagfid rejoined the Great Heathen Army and stood in the shield wall, beneath the banner of the Raven of Earthly Terror, fighting the Saxons at the Battles of Assedone and Ethandun. They lived to tell the tale of how they felt the presence of Wayland the Smith in the place to which they gave the name 'Wayland's Smithy'.

Sources

Westwood, Jennifer and Simpson, Jacqueline, *The Lore of the Land*, 2006

Taylor, Paul B. and Auden, W.H., 'The Lay of Volund', in *The Elder Edda*, 1969

❧

TWENTY ONE

FARINGDON

We continued walking west along the Ridgeway to meet the wagonette on the Lambourn to Shrivenham road, where we stopped at the Prince of Wales. Overhearing our interest in local tales, the landlord told us about Lord Oxford who, in 1752, had Shrivenham House built for his mother. During construction, Welsh miners were brought in. Sworn to secrecy, they constructed a tunnel between the new house and Becket House, home of the Barringtons, where Lord Oxford's mistress lived. Lord Oxford would visit his mother, ply her with wine till she fell asleep and was taken to bed, and then sneak into the tunnel to visit his lady.

From Shrivenham, we travelled north-west, crossing into Wiltshire, turned east at Highworth and drove through Coleshill on the Wiltshire/Berkshire boundary. Mrs Trump reminded us of the Coleshill witch who we had heard about at Brimpton. Coleshill House is the seat of the Bouverie family. Built in 1660, it is considered the finest specimen of Inigo Jones' architectural genius. The quadrangular structure retains its original character, a gem set in remarkably beautiful grounds. Further along this road is Badbury Clump, an Iron Age settlement among the trees, where we paused briefly before moving on towards our next encounter with King Alfred.

On reaching Faringdon, we drove into the Market Place and stopped outside The Bell Hotel, where we booked lunch. We then set out to explore this historic town. Faringdon was once called Feardune or Fearndun; it was the seat of the West Saxon kings, and Edward the Elder died here. The ancient castle was razed by King Stephen during the Civil War in the twelfth century, and a Cistercian priory was founded on the site of the castle by King John in 1212. At the Dissolution it was given to the Seymours and the Englefields, and has now entirely disappeared. Sir Marmaduke Rawdon garrisoned an ancient mansion near the church for Charles I. It sustained two attacks by Parliamentarian troops – one of them headed by Cromwell himself – and was one of the last places to surrender.

The Old Town Hall, in the marketplace, is an interesting building, combining a council chamber above and the town lockup beneath. Up the hill from the hotel is All Saints' Church, with its squat, square central tower and ancient graveyard. Revd Plumb discovered that the tower had originally been topped with a fine steeple, but in 1645 this had been felled. Within the church we were shown the grave of Sir Marmaduke Rawdon.

Returning to The Bell, we settled down to an excellent lunch and Professor Gaunt told us the second half of the story of King Alfred the Great:

THE RAVEN OF EARTHLY TERROR (2) – BATTLE OF ETHANDUN

After the Battle of Assedone, during six years of inconclusive clashes a pattern had emerged. The Danes, under their new leader Guthrum, occupied and fortified a Saxon town. Ælfred blockaded it and then negotiated a treaty, which Guthrum swore on the holy ring of Thor to uphold. Hostages were exchanged and the Danes left with their plunder. Later, the Danes broke the treaty, slaughtered their hostages, and moved on to the next Saxon town. During this period, neither side gained the upper hand.

Finally, unable to defeat the Saxons, the Danes withdrew to their stronghold at Gleawecestre. Ælfred spent Christmas at Cippanhamm, only 50 miles away. On the Feast of Epiphany, the Danes made a surprise attack on Cippanhamm and seized the town. Ælfred barely escaped capture. Leaping astride Epona, he galloped across the downs to his royal villa at Fearndun, where some of his scattered forces might gather, only to find the Danes were there before him.

Ælfred took a back way into the village of Fearndun and gingerly knocked on a cottage door, which was opened by a bonny, bluff housewife with flour to her elbows. Seeing a mud-splattered Saxon warrior on her doorstep, she swiftly pulled him inside and hid his white mare in a shed with the pigs. Then she left him until she finished her griddle cakes and laid them in shallow earthenware pots over the hot embers of the fire.

In her brusque way she told Ælfred, 'You can sleep by the fire if you've a mind, but I've no time to wait on you. So, while I fetch my husband you can mind the cakes on the fire, and don't let 'em burn or you'll be for it.'

While the housewife was away, Ælfred pondered on how he, a fugitive king, might restore his kingdom, but no solution came into his mind, any more than did the griddle cakes, until he heard the irate housewife's scream: 'You stupid, ungrateful oaf, you think we've food to burn in these hard times?' Ælfred had burnt the cakes. She bashed him about the head with her besom and brushed him out of the cottage, 'Get out, you lazy good-for-nothing, for burning my cakes you can sleep with the pigs.'

This was the shock Ælfred needed to see his way through. Lying beside Epona in the muck of the pigsty, he saw how the cycle of occupations, blockades, treaties made and broken, battles won and lost, had to end. It burnt and ravaged the land. It was like burning the cakes over and over, each time getting a beating. The solution was now in his mind and within his grasp.

Departing the pigsty before dawn, he galloped across the downs to the treacherous Sumorsæte marshes, where some of his forces were gathered and the Danes were loath to venture. He fortified the monastic settlement at Æthelingaeg and sat out the winter, refining his plans for a final showdown with the Danes. During this time, in the guise of a minstrel, he visited Guthrum at Cippanhamm, where he overheard his enemy's plans and discovered the Danish strength.

When all was ready, Ælfred rode out from Æthelingaeg one late spring morning on his white mare Epona, with a small band of hardened veterans, to begin quietly gathering the fyrd of Sumorsæte, Wiltunscir, Hamtunscir and Bearrucscir. A mighty host mustered at Ethandun to confront the Viking foe, which came out from Cippanhamm to face them.

Amid the ranks of Danish warriors, Ubbe stood a foot above the rest, his cruel eyes shot with hatred and rage. Beside him the Raven of Earthly Terror was raised high, crowing over the Saxons for their past failures in battle. All the same, Guthrum was perturbed by the strength of the Saxon army, when his own forces were so diminished: Bacsecq was slain, Ivar the Boneless was lost in the mire, Halfdan Ragnarsson had taken his forces to quell rebellion in the north.

Shield walls were raised and clashed together. With overwhelming numbers, the Saxons broke the Danes' shield wall with much slaughter and took to hand-to-hand fighting with swords and axes. Where the affray was thickest there fought the giant Ubbe, wielding a heavy axe, thundering the curses of Thor, striking dismay and despair into the hearts of the most battle-hardened Saxon warriors and cutting them down like a scythe in ripe corn.

Not so Æthelwulf, Ealdorman of Wessex. Watching Ubbe, he saw how the giant used his great height and thundering imprecations to overawe his adversaries before hacking them down with savage force, yet without guile or craft or cleverness. He was simply a brute. Æthelwulf slowly approached Ubbe, shouting to other Saxons around, 'This one is mine!'

Bellowing Thor's curses, Ubbe swung his axe around his head, preparing to strike. Æthelwulf calmly took a stance, left foot forward, right leg braced against the ground, raising his shield, standing firmly to receive the blow. The axe embedded itself in the lime wood shield, and before Ubbe could wrest it out, Æthelwulf reached under his shield and stabbed him in the groin. Ubbe fell to his knees screaming in agony. Æthelwulf stepped sideways and in a single stroke sliced off Ubbe's head, then hefted it high for the Danes to see.

Ubbe's standard bearer, stunned to see his lord so swiftly slain, stared aghast for a moment then sought to flee, before he too was cut down. The Raven of Earthly Terror, woven by the Norns and symbol of Thor's divine power and the rightness of the Viking cause, slipped from the standard bearer's dead hands and was trampled into the churned earth of Wessex.

With the loss of their greatest warrior and the Raven of Earthly Terror, the disheartened Danes fled from the field. Ælfred had carefully briefed the chiefs of his war bands to exercise discipline and hold back from hot pursuit, but to follow the Danes some way behind, allowing them to return to Cippanhamm. Then he surrounded the town at a distance of 500 yards. All the food within this perimeter, which the Danes might send out sorties to obtain, was removed. Ælfred waited. After two weeks the starving Danes sued for peace, offering hostages, their usual tactic.

Ælfred met with Guthrum, stating his terms: 'It is Christ who has won this victory. Thor has been utterly defeated and the symbol of his might, the Raven of Earthly Terror, has been trodden into the earth. So now, to bring a final end to this conflict, you must make an oath to serve Christ alone and receive the sacrament of baptism, you and all your earls, and I, even I, shall be your father in God.'

Not only did Guthrum have no choice, but also he was genuinely moved by the solemnity of the baptism service and the moral power of his new faith. He freely agreed to leave the Kingdom of Wessex forever and to live in peace as Ælfred's spiritual son.

As Ælfred had known all along, he too had no choice. Now, in good conscience, he too must relinquish the old religion and serve Christ alone. For a spell, he dwelt wistfully upon the sacred thorn tree, how it had been a true portent of challenges ahead and the promise of betterment once these had been faced and overcome. Then, he let the old religion go. Ælfred had achieved the objective he had set as he lay in the muck of the pigsty – not simply to win a victory but to win a lasting peace. Thereafter, he has been known as a Christian hero and, for some, a Christian saint.

SOURCE

Summers, Revd W.H. and Peake, Harold (Eds), *The Story of Hungerford in Berkshire*, 1926

Berkshire folklore cites Eddington in Berkshire as the site of the Battle of Ethandun on 12 May 878, though there are other claimants; otherwise, the historical aspects of the story are generally accurate.

In particular, the conversion of Guthrum to Christianity, with Ælfred as his father in God, was a significant turning point in the long-running conflict between Saxons and Danes.

The folk tale of Ælfred burning the cakes at Faringdon provides a metaphor for the shift which Ælfred sees as necessary, and is therefore the turning point of the story of the Battle of Ethandun.

TWENTY-TWO

EAST HAGBOURNE

Refreshed and ready for the next leg of our journey, we travelled south-east towards Wantage, but soon turned left and continued through Hatford, the name of which comes, according to Mr Vanderpump's informant, from King Alfred and his men stopping at the ford to drink on their return from fighting the Danes, fighting being thirsty work. They had no vessels to drink from so used their hats, thus the name Hatford.

Passing the turning for Stanford-in-the-Vale, we turned right to Charney Bassett, with its ancient manor house. Here we turned south, then east again, through West and East Hanney, and on to Steventon. We stopped here briefly to stretch our legs and admire the tree-lined ancient causeway. We saw no trace of the castle, built in 1281, or the Benedictine priory founded in the time of Henry I.

From Steventon we travelled south to the crossroads at Rowstock, where, about twenty years ago, Captain George Holford had a strange encounter. When posted in London, Captain Holford frequently walked from his barracks in the capital to visit his uncle, Sir Robert Loyd-Lindsay, at Lockinge House, starting in the early morning and arriving in time for dinner. On this afternoon, as he approached the crossroads, he saw two men struggling together. One man was on the ground and the other had a knife and was poised to stab his fallen opponent. Captain Holford rushed forward to stop this act, only to find himself alone …

At this crossroads, we turned east towards Harwell and the Hagbournes. East Hagbourne is celebrated for its cherry orchards and watercress beds. There is an ancient market cross surmounting lofty steps, and here Richard Corbett, Dean of Christchurch, Oxford, turned ballad seller. He and his friends were drinking in the local alehouse one market day, when they overheard the complaints of a ballad seller who could get no custom for his wares. Discarding his gown and borrowing the balladeer's leather jacket and satchel of broadsheets, the cleric mounted the steps of the cross and began to sing. His fine tenor voice soon attracted an audience and ballad sales followed thick and fast.

The church here is one of the best in the county, Revd Plumb informed us, the peal of eight bells being remarkably good. From the church and cross we walked down to the Fleur de Lis for light refreshments. Another helpful landlord introduced us to a gentleman who told us the story of Bob Appleford and his pig.

Bob Appleford's Pig

There's a saying in Berkshire, addressed to anyone who's a nosy parker, 'Tha'll ne'er get Bob Appleford's pig.'

Bob Appleford lived in the village of East Hagbourne. He had a very fine Berkshire boar. It was 6ft long, 50in high, and weighed in at no less than 1,200lb. It was sandy-red all over. It had pointed ears and its curly tail had six twirls to its spiral. It was Smithfield Champion three years running and had sired Smithfield Champions every year for the last twelve years.

You couldn't go into any tavern in western Berkshire without hearing yokels talking about 'Bob Appleford's pig' and cogitating on the secret of Bob's success with his pigs, and especially how he'd got such a champion porker.

But Bob'd never tell, however much his mates tried to wheedle it out of him. In fact he threw out a challenge, 'I'll give away yon porker to anyone as can prove he's always minded 'is own business, not like you nosy parkers.'

Well, all the nosy parkers for miles around tried it on, but they were too well known, as nosy parkers always are, and they went

away empty-handed, so to speak. Mind, Bob were a canny lad
and charged a thruppenny bit for every try, 'To help wi't feed bill,'
he said.

One day an old farmer from Didcot way came over for a try.
He were a taciturn old beggar; grunted mostly, like Bob's boar. Bob
Appleford proudly took the old boy to show him the pig, 'A very
fine beast, as I'm sure you'll agree.'

''Appen!' grunted the old farmer. 'Big, any road.'

Bob felt a bit deflated at this response, and was a mite too quick
to defend his own, 'Yes, a very fine beast. Smithfield Champion
three years running and sired a dozen more, I'll 'ave you know.'

'Ay, reet,' was the grunted reply. 'But what o't bacon?'

Bob laughed, a bit nervous like. 'Bacon? You want me to carve a
slice off t'owd pig? We feed him t' best victuals to mek t' bacon an'
'am sweet as 'oney.'

'Oh, ah!' said the old codger, 'that'd be?'

'Well, I mix up …' began Bob, his big gob running away with itself, before he bethought himself and stopped, '… any road, that'd be my business and not yourn. Good day to ye.'

As the old farmer walked off and Bob pocketed his thruppenny bit, Bob muttered to himself, 'Nosy parker!'

So, if you've a mind to poke your nose into another folk's business, just remember this thought, 'Tha'll ne'er get Bob Appleford's pig.'

SOURCE

Lowsley, Major B., *Berkshire Words and Phrases*, 1888

Follow quiet lanes to East and West Hagbourne and discover delightfully pretty villages.

BLEWBURY

From East Hagbourne, we travelled south to Blewbury, through the cherry orchards for which this area is famous. Blewbury is a charming village and we left the wagonette to explore, while Revd Plumb went to see the vicar, Jacob Macdonald, an old friend who had offered to accommodate us for the night. The church is indeed the centre of village life here. Close by is a farm that was once a moated manor house. Narrow lanes and paths around the church are lined with pretty cottages, their gardens rivalling each other for pride of place in the eyes of their neighbours.

Chapel Lane, leading down to a corner of the remaining part of the moat, is named for the neat brick chapel built at the end some thirty years ago, replacing an older and less sturdy structure. In 1746, John Wesley visited and preached here. Many were clearly moved by his sermon, but the landlord of the Red Lion was probably not among the congregation.

We rejoined Revd Plumb at the church, an ancient building of stone, flint and rubble, much altered over the years since its Saxon beginnings. The mixed styles give it the feel of a building that has grown to meet the needs of the community it serves, and the vicar reinforced this impression as he showed us the interesting tombs, monuments and brasses within. Revd Macdonald informed us that it was here that St Birinus began his conversion of the Midlands; he succeeded in persuading the local chief to convert to Christianity when he preached on Churn Knob in 634. We then retired to the vicarage, where we had a simple, wholesome meal, after which he promised us a tale that was touching and true. Just then there was a knock on the door, and in came a man wearing the most extraordinary hat and coat, which looked as if he had just stolen them from a scarecrow. He proceeded to tell the story of a former vicar of the parish:

THE MISER OF BLEWBURY

Reverend Morgan Jones, curate-in-charge of St Michael's Church, Blewbury, held a simple maxim: 'Bread, bacon and tea are all a man requires, two necessities and one luxury.' The maxim seemed to serve him well, for he was always in excellent health and throughout his long ministry he was only absent from Sunday services on two occasions.

Reverend Morgan Jones limited his expenditure on bread, bacon and tea to a modest 2s 6d per week, affording him little for luxury.

Reverend Morgan Jones thought visiting his parishioners on a regular basis for friendly discourse was an essential part of his ministry, and he was punctilious in this observance. One of his regulars was Farmer Johnson, from whom the curate bought his bacon. He would visit the Johnsons just before teatime to order 4lb of bacon, and these courteous country folk would invite him in to tea. The curate was well-versed in every aspect of country and ecclesiastical life and could discourse at length on these subjects, until it was time for supper in fact – a fine rack of the farmer's lamb perhaps, or a plump chicken, with mashed turnips and roast potatoes. 'Why don't you stay for supper,' Goodwife Johnson would say, with just the tiniest edge to her courtesy.

Reverend Morgan Jones would visit Farmer Johnson again to collect his bacon, and he would enjoy the same hospitality. He would visit again to pay for the bacon, reflecting to himself how 2s 6d per week can go quite a long way and how much his flock must value his diligent parochial visits. He was a dedicated parish visitor.

Reverend Morgan Jones possessed a black ecclesiastical hat which had seen better days. He lengthened the life of his hat by sewing onto it the brim of a brown hat he found in a hedge, which had been discarded by a tramp. The black overcoat which

he had when he took up his curacy he made to serve until the end of his ministry by judicious patching and mending with miscellaneous scraps of fabric, and by cutting pieces from the tail to repair the upper part.

Reverend Morgan Jones was averse to any form of extravagance, which included paper on which to write his sermons. He wrote these on whatever scraps of paper came to hand: the backs of old marriage banns, bills of sale, old proclamations, tax papers, brown wrapping paper, and the backs of used sandpaper. When his Rector, Revd John Keble, wrote to him on parish matters, using both sides of the paper, Revd Jones turned the letter upside down and wrote a funeral sermon between the lines. Over 1,000 sermons he wrote on these heterogeneous, scavenged morsels of paper.

Reverend Morgan Jones delivered his most powerful and passionate sermon at the time of the Battle of Waterloo, when loyal addresses were delivered from every pulpit, exhorting the congregation to subscribe generously to the widows and orphans of those slain in battle. Hearing his stirring words, the greater part of Revd Morgan's congregation openly wept and reached for their pocket books. The following day, a collector for the widows and orphans fund came to his door, expecting a generous donation. At first he demurred, and when pressed handed over half a crown. When strongly pressed further, he openly wept as he handed over another half crown. When strenuously pressed some more he thundered, 'Have you forgotten my sermon of yesterday and the liberal sum it produced? There was my contribution to this glorious cause, I will give no more!' and peremptorily turned the collector from his door.

Reverend Morgan Jones never married, though there were two single ladies to whom he tipped his tatty, ecclesiastical hat, believing, as he was neither spendthrift nor profligate, that he was a desirable matrimonial prospect. Neither lady reciprocated, spinsterhood seeming a more congenial option than death by starvation in marriage to Revd Jones.

Reverend Morgan Jones received a stipend of £50 per annum, supplemented by £30 per annum from a small property he had inherited from a relative. His remaining income was the 2s 6d per week surplice fee on which he contrived to live. Remarkably, with compound interest his account stood at a princely £18,000 when he reached eighty years of age.

Reverend Morgan Jones longed, at that great age, to return to his native Wales, and to see out his days restfully at Llandovery, the place of his birth. He wrote this to a niece in those parts. She had a similar family trait: an eye to a pecuniary advantage. When she arrived in Blewbury, and saw his beggarly state, her thoughts towards him were less than friendly as she contemplated her wasted investment in coach fares. She began to make excuses: 'Llandovery is a long way for an old man to travel on draughty coaches, and the journey is costly. I say, where the tree falls, there it has to lie. It really doesn't signify where you will one day be buried. You can see out your days here with people you know.' She would have cut her losses and departed on the next coach, leaving him to die in solitude, had she not met Farmer Johnson in the village and heard from him the rumours of what the miser was worth. Returning to Revd Jones, she changed her tune. 'Oh, all right then, we'll set out for Llandovery on tomorrow's coach.'

Reverend Morgan Jones ended his days soon after his return to Llandovery, and his niece inherited the small fortune he had skimped and scraped and saved for all his ministry, denying himself life's simplest comforts and pleasures. Yet, for all his parsimony and miserly sponging off his parishioners, they found they missed his regular parish visits and genial discourses, and many wept openly at his valedictory sermon. Indeed, one family retains to this day the rags of his hat and coat, displaying these relics in a glass case as a bizarre remembrance of his ministry, for he was not the sole eccentric in the village.

The Revd Plumb warned us that the vicar would take nothing for his hospitality, so we asked what local charity would benefit from a donation and duly put money towards the upkeep of the school, the Revd Macdonald being firmly of the opinion that education was the best way to prevent poverty.

SOURCE

Salmon, Miss L., *Untravelled Berkshire*, 1909

TWENTY-FOUR

ALDWORTH

From Blewbury, we took the main road that skirts the steeper hills, dropping down to the Thames at Streatley. There has been a river crossing here since at least Roman times. We turned west again, heading uphill, travelling through Westridge Green and Hungerford Green before arriving at Aldworth for our next story.

The manor belonged to the de la Beche family. The church contains nine effigies. The great stone carvings above each tomb suggest that the men of the de la Beche family were very tall, which has led to them being dubbed the Aldworth Giants. Locals told us that 'four Johns' are buried in Aldworth Church: John Long, John Strong, John Never-Afraid, and John Ever-Afraid.

These figures have been legendary as far back as the reign of Queen Elizabeth, who made a journey on horseback to see them. There were originally ten effigies. A Royalist Colonel, Richard Symonds, passing through Aldworth during the Civil War, noted in his diary that a parchment identifying all ten effigies had been removed in the days of Queen Elizabeth, and remarked on a tomb in the exterior wall. Though vandalised by Cromwell's men not long after the Colonel's visit, the unique Aldworth Giants remain very impressive.

The churchyard is circular and surrounded by holly bushes, suggesting that this was a holy site before Christianity stamped its mark on the landscape. Near the path is an ancient yew tree, some 25ft in girth, which, according to the locals, is over 1,500 years old – the oldest in the country.

Having examined the monuments and carvings within and without the church, we retired to The Bell, a fine rustic alehouse, where we sat and drank coffee while listening to Mr Rowland recounting the fate of John Ever-Afraid:

THE ALDWORTH GIANTS AND THE FATE OF JOHN EVER-AFRAID

Lord de la Beche, haughty and proud, stands beside an ancient yew tree within a circle of holly trees, glorying in his new demesne on the high Berkshire Downs. He determines – on this site, which he regards as a place of pagan worship – to build a church to his god – and to himself and his family. He will build a castle to project his power over the land. He will turn the local people into bondsmen.

The yew tree has marked and guarded this holy ground for 100 generations, seeding and reseeding itself. Within its circle of holly trees, the yew has been a place of worship and pilgrimage for countless generations of local people. The tree stands in the hamlet of Aldworth, barely 3 miles from the great confluence of three ancient routes as old as the tree's own lineage: Ridgeway, Icknield Way, and the River Thames.

The old yew has seen many peoples sweep over this landscape, sometimes to remain, latterly Romans, Saxons, Danes, and now Normans, bringing their own religious practices. Yet the remnants of local people, those who have known this land from the beginning, remain in their hearts true to the old religion of Mother Earth and Father Sun. Though they may pay lip-service to the gods of whomsoever their current masters may be, they perceive always the old religion nestling beneath.

These faithful people know to respect Earth and Sun, know the giving and taking of Sun's warmth and Earth's fruit with each turn of the seasons, and that Mother Earth and Father Sun fulfil all of their needs.

These people also know that when Earth and Sun are not respected, dark forces are released, bringing mayhem, fear, bloodshed, the rapacious greed of men. Ever and always, these faithful people turn to their sacred yew – which stretches its branches towards the Sun and spreads its roots deep and wide into the Earth. They honour the yew's ancient wisdom and power; they offer thanks and seek its protection from dark forces.

Lord de la Beche was a giant of a man, 7ft tall some say, and mighty in battle. Succeeding generations of the de la Beche family were as mighty as he. One by one, they fought for their king, or against him, or served in the high offices of the land; and, one by one, they died and were buried in the family church.

The yew continued to thrive while many generations of de la Beche turned to dust. Then came Robert de la Beche. After being knighted by King Edward I, Sir Robert desired not only to be a giant in life but also to be a giant in death. He laid down that, after his death, a full-sized effigy of himself, in plated armour and surcoat, with a dwarf at his foot to accentuate his giant size, should be raised in the church over his sarcophagus.

And, in the way he was immortalised, so were succeeding giants, two of them having their wives lying with them. In all, ten effigies were raised about the church. Four of these ten were called John de la Beche. In view of their immense size and strength and fearlessness in battle, three of these were named, respectively, John Long, John Strong, and John Never-Afraid. This story is about the fourth John de la Beche.

The fourth John de la Beche was a younger son, without title or estate. He could have been a soldier or a priest or a servant of the state, but felt no affinity with any of these professions. Yet, he did feel an affinity with the sacred yew; he somehow knew how the yew indifferently dispensed its power between the light and the dark. He learned, little by little, how to draw upon the dark forces and use them in secret to gain wealth and power over other men.

When John de la Beche summoned the ancient forces of the dark, they appeared to him in a form which he could understand, not as they would appear to those who have known this land from the beginning. They appeared in the form of the Devil, just as church stained-glass windows depict him, with ram horns and bloody fangs, cloven hooves and forked tail, fierce red eyes and sewer breath.

John de la Beche was undaunted by the Devil's dread presence, for he was of the same stock as John Never-Afraid, and commanded the Devil to serve him.

'Well,' sneered the Devil, 'I'm willing to make a deal with you, but what can you poor mortal possibly offer in return to such as I?'

'I shall give you the souls of the bondsmen under my control,' replied John de la Beche. 'I will send them into battle, and as they fall and die without the ministrations of the Church, you can snatch them from the field. All you have to do is to climb to the top of this yew tree, and write the names of all the souls you espy in your book, and they shall be yours for eternity.'

'We have a bargain!' screamed the Devil, his lewd horns aquiver and his lascivious lips slavering with anticipation, as he scaled the yew with some difficulty; hooves provide a poor foothold for balancing on branches. When he made the summit of the tree, there was not a soul in sight. The people had perceived the presence of the dark forces and had hidden from them in Mother Earth.

Meanwhile, John de la Beche had taken his knife and carved the sign of the cross in the yew tree's trunk. True to his disguise, the Devil, as Christ's adversary, could not pass the sign of the cross, and was captive in the tree.

'Well, well,' mused the Devil. 'We had a deal and now we have an impasse, if you will allow me such a devilishly apt pun. I am willing to sit in this tree for all of eternity, but you, mortal, will die, the tree will heal over in time and allow me to pass, then I shall have your soul. If they bury you in this churchyard or if they bury you beneath one of your ridiculous effigies in the church, I shall have your soul for the whole of eternity.'

'I suppose you have me there,' said John de la Beche, sadly. 'If you play with the fires of Hell you are sure to be burnt. But, you will surely serve me, Devil, and fulfil all my desires as long as I live. So, it will be worth it. And I agree to your new bargain. When I die, if they bury me in this churchyard or beneath my effigy in the church, you shall have my soul for the rest of eternity.' So saying, he took his knife again to cut out the sign of the cross from the tree and allow the Devil to descend.

And so it was: the Devil served John de la Beche all the days of his life and all his greedy desires were fulfilled. But, beneath the veil of a spurious confession, John de la Beche gave careful instructions to the priest: when he died he was to be buried not in the churchyard and not in the church, but in an alcove cut into the church's outer wall.

At the moment of death, a smug smile spread over John de la Beche's ravaged features, as he thought how he had so cunningly defeated the Devil and escaped his eternal clutches. A moment later, his soul soared from his body. But where was it to go? He was not allowed to ascend into Heaven, because he had sold his soul to the Devil. He could not descend into Hell, for that would be against the bargain he and the Devil had made, though he would have met many of his relatives there.

So, the soul of John de la Beche is doomed to spend eternity alone, wandering the arid wastes between Heaven and Hell. In that limitless void, he eternally suffers a fearful anguish more terrible than the torments of Hell, which is the ghastly sense of being perpetually on the brink of not existing at all.

Gathered within the circle of holly trees, beside the immemorial yew, the people who have known this land from the beginning sought a new name for John de la Beche, along with John Long, John Strong, and John Never-Afraid. The fourth John, whose memorial lies neither in nor out of the church, they call John Ever-Afraid.

SOURCES

Westwood, Jennifer and Simpson, Jacqueline, *The Lore of the Land*, 2006

Gray, Edward William, *The History and Antiquities of Newbury and its Environs*, 1839

◈

This is Colonel Symond's account of the Aldworth Giants folk tale:

May 2, 1644. Aldworth. In ye E. end of ye S. yle did hang a table fairly written in parchment of all ye names of ye Family of de la Beche, but ye Earle of Leicester coming with ye Queen Elizabeth in progresse tooke it down to show it her, and it was neuer broughte againe. Ye common People call ye statue under ye outside of ye Churche John Euerafraid and say further that he gaue his soule to ye Diuel if euer he was buried either in Churche or In Churchyard, so he was buried under the Church Wall under an Arche.

TWENTY-FIVE

PANGBOURNE

From Aldworth, we drove south-east towards Upper Basildon. Just before we reached the village, Mr Cleave pointed out Tomb Farm, where Old Nobes had built his own tomb in which to be buried, being a Nonconformist or having fallen out with the local vicar. The tomb has the year 1692 over the door. Once he was entombed, the door was to be locked and the key posted through a small aperture in the door, thus preventing any disturbance of his chosen final resting place. However, rumours spread that Nobes was a miser and had been buried with all his money, which led to the tomb being broken open by some local with a ploughshare. From that day the ghost of Old Nobes, on his white horse, has haunted the district.

We passed through Upper Basildon and continued down into the valley to reach Pangbourne, entering the village by the church. This is the place where the River Pang joins the Thames, hence the name. A toll bridge crosses the Thames at this point. Roman remains, including a beautiful and interesting mosaic, were discovered here in 1840 during excavations for the Great Western Railway. Brunel promised to preserve the mosaic, which might have made an interesting feature in the new station building, but this promise, and the mosaic, were broken. Luckily Messrs Grissel and Peto made a drawing before this act of wanton vandalism took place.

The manor was founded by Henry I, and in 1126 he gave it to Reading Abbey. We lunched at the Cross Keys, a pleasant hostelry by the church. Harold Benjamin thought this was an apt place to begin a tale of cruelty culminating at Reading Abbey.

TRIAL BY COMBAT (1) –
REMINISCENCE OF A VILLAINOUS LIFE

Field of Combat

Henry de Essex stands in the early morning light at the edge of the field of combat and surveys the festive scene, with flags and pennants crackling in the stiff river breeze. de Essex sees the larger boats moored to the eyot, close to the River Gate of the Royal and Noble Monastery of Radingia, dressed overall in bright bunting.

He sees the tall dais erected for King Henry II, surmounted by a rich scarlet canopy with orange trim. Above it flies the royal coat of arms: Two Facing Lions Rampant, Or, On a Field of Scarlet. He sees the dais erected for Abbot Roger of Radingia, almost as grand as the King's, surmounted by a canopy of blue with the Abbot's crest.

He sees, at the edge of the field of combat, his opponent's pavilion, gaudily striped in yellow and blue and embellished by yellow and blue streamers, busy in the brisk breeze. Beside him is his own pavilion, boldly striped in scarlet and orange.

He feels wryly proud that all of this, this festive field, is for him, marking out the high esteem in which he is held by the great men of the realm; were he not one of the mightiest men in England, he would have received a summary execution for treason.

At the same time, this field may mark the grave moment of his igno-miny and death. Soon enough, on this field he will meet his accuser and adversary Robert de Montfort in a Trial by Combat.

As he scans the field of combat, he reminisces on the strands of his life which have converged to bring him to this place and time.

Discrediting of Robert de Vere

Henry de Essex knows himself to be an ambitious, vicious, ruthless man without remorse or moral scruple. He remembers, with a cold heart and a sour smile, the historic enmity between himself and Robert de Montfort.

༺

Robert de Montfort's sister Adeline became wife to Robert de Vere, by which her husband received the honour of the office of Royal

Constable. But Robert de Vere was no match for the scheming mind of Henry de Essex, who, by innuendo, rumour and bald deceit brought Robert into disrepute and wrenched from him the office of Royal Constable, a position of great dignity at the Court of King Henry II.

This brought de Essex the power he craved. As Royal Constable he was a close advisor to King Henry II, quartermaster-general to the army and King Henry's Court, and Royal Standard Bearer.

And, in Robert de Montfort, the usurping of his brother-in-law's office engendered a rancorous resentment, like a serpent coiled in his bowels, awaiting its time to strike.

Treachery at the Battle of Ewloe

Henry de Essex remembers with some bitterness the dishonour and disgrace he suffered, after the Battle of Ewloe, at the hands of rascally Robert de Montfort, which even then almost robbed him of life.

It all began when Owain Gwynedd ap Gruffydd, Prince of North Wales, confiscated the estates of his brother Cadwaladr and banished him from Wales. When Cadwaladr, taking refuge at the English Court, implored King Henry's aid to recover his lands, the King saw an opportunity to re-establish English hegemony over the whole of Wales.

Feudal levies were raised, knights were commissioned, and an expedition was launched into North Wales, supported by a great fleet of ships commanded by Madog ap Maredudd, Prince of Powys. With youthful enthusiasm, and with his Standard Bearer, Henry de Essex, close behind, King Henry marched up the Dee estuary hoping to take Owain by surprise. Instead, Owain ambushed the royal army at Ewloe in a narrow, wooded valley, routing it completely, with King Henry himself narrowly avoiding capture.

In the fog of armed conflict, Henry de Essex became separated from his king. Then he heard a cry go up: 'The King is slain; the King is slain.' As Standard Bearer, it was his honourable duty to search for the King and serve him in whatever way was possible, if only to save his corpse from the ravages of the victorious Welsh; he had sworn allegiance to his liege lord to lay down his life for him. Honour, duty and allegiance not being qualities which de Essex enthusiastically espoused, he cast the Two Facing Lions Rampant, Or, On a Field of Scarlet into the churned mire of the narrow valley and fled.

It turned out the King was not dead. He rallied the remainder of his army, and bravely cut his way through the ambush with such vigour that Owain was forced to retreat into the Snowdon hills. With King Henry encamped in the refortified Rhuddlan Castle, Owain feared being hemmed in between the English army and Madog ap Maredudd's great fleet. He sued for peace, did homage to King Henry, reinstated Cadwaladr, and provided hostages for his future loyalty.

Once the conflict was settled, the serpent in Robert de Montfort's guts seized its moment to strike. Robert knelt before the King and boldly charged Henry de Essex with cowardice in the face of the enemy and treason for abandoning the King in the heat of battle, casting the Royal Standard into the muck. The moment proved to be poorly chosen, for, fired by battle and flushed with victory, the King was feeling magnanimous; he dismissed the charges and acquitted Henry de Essex of his misdeeds with a regal wave of the hand. As Robert bowed to his king and withdrew, the serpent of resentment coiled more tightly in his bowels.

Defrauding of St Edmund

Faced with a Trial by Combat, Henry de Essex feels poorly recompensed by the King for the distinguished service he rendered during the King's expedition against Toulouse.

He recalls that, alone amongst the nobles, he and Chancellor Thomas Becket had faithfully accepted the task of protecting the King's territories against King Louis VII of France and his ally Count Raymond Berengar IV of Barcelona. Afterwards, though, he had been foully pilloried for misappropriation of St Edmund's revenues, as if everyone else wasn't lining their pockets as well as he.

King Edmund of East Anglia had raised the Christian standard against the incursion of Ivar the Boneless and his brothers Ubbe and Halfdan, and their Great Heathen Army of Vikings, into his realm. Defeated in battle at Thetford, Edmund was taken to the church at Haegelisdun. Edmund was first tied to a tree and used by Ivar's archers for target practice. Then, deeply riddled with arrows, he was torn from the trunk and beheaded. His head was thrown into a thicket. His body was left to rot for a year before Edmund's men could recover it. Whilst searching for the head, they heard the King's voice calling to them, 'Here! Here! Here!'

Edmund's men gently reunited his head with his body and buried him in the churchyard at Haegelisdun. After Edmund had been canonised for his defence of Christendom against the pagan horde, his martyrdom, and the miracle of his calling head, St Edmund was reburied in a shrine at Bury St Edmunds, which became a place of devotion and pilgrimage.

Those Norman lords who had settled in East Anglia before the conquest honoured the Saxon St Edmund. Their families continued to honour him, enlarging and adorning his resting place with rich gifts. de Essex's great-grandfather, Robert Fitz-Wimark, had settled in East Anglia in the time of Edward the Confessor, and had held the dying king in his arms.

Despite these precedents, de Essex despised the reverence afforded to St Edmund and flatly defrauded him. By lawyer's tricks, tort, threats and brute violence, he diverted much of the revenue from St Edmund's Court to the treasury of his own Lailand Hundred. By such and by such he drew to himself the growing disfavour of his peers.

Murder of Gilbert de Cereville

Henry de Essex turns his mind, somewhat reluctantly, to his wife Cecily. She is a voluptuous beauty, passionate, with a voracious appetite. With her green eyes, her long hair, raven-black, the soft dark down upon her, all it takes is the curl of a lip, the swing of a hip, to drive men to distraction. These were the reasons de Essex married her. Yet, he proved unable to satisfy her insatiable desire. As he thinks of her, rage and shame struggle together in his breast.

❧

During de Essex's frequent absences, with the King or with the army as quartermaster-general, Cecily turned enthusiastically to his knights. The knights took their pleasure and sniggeringly despised their lord. de Essex knew this, yet he resolutely turned his face away in shame from such knowing.

None of the knights were immune to Cecily's beguilement. All it took was the curl of a lip, the swing of a hip, to drive them to distraction. None, save one, Gilbert de Cereville. Gilbert was the most loyal of knights, the most honourable. Cecily used all her voluptuous charms on him, all her woman's wiles and cunning stratagems, and all the while he held himself apart. She became so furiously obsessed with him that one day she blurted out to de Essex that Gilbert de Cereville had tried to make love to her. In that moment, all of de Essex's pent-up cuckold wrath was released and focused upon Gilbert.

de Essex had Gilbert seized, beaten and chained up in a deep dungeon, without light, without food, and with only a flask of water, so that his slow torment was as prolonged as possible. It was many days before an emaciated Gilbert de Cereville died of starvation, an innocent, loyal and honourable knight, to satisfy de Essex's bitterness and spite.

When the full story of Cecily's part in Gilbert's shocking and brutal murder by de Essex trickled out, society quickly dubbed her 'Potiphar's wife'.

❧

Thus does Henry de Essex, as he approaches his Trial by Combat, remember and justify to himself his many villainous deeds.

SOURCES

Hurry, Jamieson B., *The Trial by Combat of Henry de Essex and Robert de Montfort at Reading Abbey*, 1919

Childs, W.M., *The Story of the Town of Reading*, 1905

If you go to Reading Museum and Art Gallery, you will be able to see the painting *The Trial by Combat of Henry de Essex and Robert de Montfort* by Harry Morley. The setting and account of the Trial by Combat are drawn from Harry Morley's painting and Jamieson Hurry's book. The flashbacks describing the circumstances of Henry de Essex's past crimes are based largely on the book

TWENTY-SIX

SULHAM WOODS

We drove out of Pangbourne discussing how de Essex's tale might end, but Harold remained smilingly and stubbornly silent on the subject. We took the road south to Tidmarsh, where we turned east through Sulham and up the hill into the woods. Here we were a little north-west of Calcot woods, in which was enacted the climax of a strange and romantic tale which Mr Rowland wanted to share with us.

Fight Me or Wed Me

Her mother always told her, 'Frances, you are a wilful child.' Just how true this was was revealed when she was orphaned at thirteen.

Frances already possessed beauty and grace, wit and wild spirit. And an indomitable will! Her auburn hair flowed down to her shoulders. She was tall and straight. As she watched her mother being laid in the ground, she determined to be her own woman, controlled by no one, owned by no one. She was now a wealthy heiress, daughter of the late Sir William Kendrick Bart., and had every intention of being master of her own affairs.

Of course, her mother's last will and testament had imposed guardians upon her, Dr James Brewer and a Reading lawyer, John Dalby; but, the doctor was a bachelor who loved an easy life and had no resistance to Frances' demands, and the lawyer was easily beguiled by Frances' charms. So, soon after her mother's death, Frances purchased her own residence, Calcot Park, and moved there from the family home along with her chosen servants.

A woman of spirit, Frances eschewed the gentle arts in which she had been schooled as a child: playing the spinet, painting water colours and embroidering samplers. Now, she rode to hounds with a fierce enthusiasm, shot game with startling accuracy, and fenced with the flair of a Spanish fencing master, with rapier, sabre, English broadsword, and her favourite weapon, the backsword[15]. With her strong and supple wrists, an eye for her opponent's body language, a firm but relaxed grip, and her swift wits, the flexible backsword became a potent blade. Thus, she showed the world just how much she was her own woman and master of her own affairs.

The young men of the county flocked around her at every ball and soirée, at every hunt and point-to-point, jostling to gain her attention, and perhaps, as she approached marriage-able age, to win her hand, for with beauty and wealth she seemed to them to be a fine prize. She encouraged them, flirted with them indiscriminately, but gave none her favour. Privately, she called them primping, periwigged puppies, knowing none could match her passionate spirit, for what they most lusted after was her wealth.

The early spring wedding of Frances' friend Mary was a splen-did affair, with all the county in their finest outfits, and afterwards Frances opened her home at Calcot Park to receive all the guests. As per usual the preening puppies gathered around Frances, prais-ing her beauty with increasingly competitive extravagance.

Benjamin Child's first sight of Frances had been in the church as she attended her friend Mary during her wedding, deftly strok-ing a wrinkle from her gown, straightening a bow, tucking in a curl. He had known many beautiful women, but here was one with such self-assurance, such sureness of touch and poise in her movements, such contained confidence; a thrill of passion shivered through his body and pierced his heart. 'Tush!' he said. 'I shall have her, whoever she is, whatever her station, I shall win her.' How wrong he was.

Later, when he entered the hall at Calcot Park, he saw the unknown woman again, across the room, tall and straight, sur-rounded by slack-wristed young men bowing and scraping like a grove of spring saplings. He would keep his distance, patiently await his moment. When he saw a tub of oysters at a nearby corner table, his eyes gleamed with a familiar pleasure. He sat at the corner table, picked up the oyster knife, and began his wedding breakfast.

Frances caught the man's quick glance as he entered the hall, saw him turn away, saw him sit down to oysters. He was not like her fawning suitors. For sure he was neither tall nor especially handsome, yet he seemed more self-aware, more self-possessed in his studied indifference, and strangely attractive. He intrigued her and this drew her to him.

Frances moved away from her yapping puppies to find Mary, and hooking her arm in hers said, 'Let us do a tour of the hall together and talk with the guests.' With gentle greetings and affectionate embraces, with Mary in tow, with exquisite stealth, Frances sidled towards the corner table where the unknown man was still intent on eating oysters. When close enough, she addressed him boldly, 'Sire, I do not believe we have been introduced.' Suddenly aware of her friend's ploy, and with a quick glance at the two young people, Mary unhooked her arm and slipped away.

Benjamin's moment had come. He looked up at her. She lifted her chin with a defiant flourish. He held her gaze whilst lifting the oyster knife and prising open an oyster, feeling the pull of its muscle, the resistance. Still holding her gaze, with the oyster in the palm of his right hand, he palmed half a lemon in his left and squeezed it over the oyster, which he handed to her. 'Have an oyster with me.'

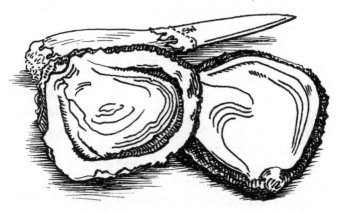

He watched as she accepted the oyster and put it to her lips. He watched as she slowly sucked the oyster into her mouth. He watched as the oyster slipped down her throat. By that time, whilst still holding her gaze, he had prised open another oyster, squeezed lemon onto it, and now handed it to her without a word spoken. As she consumed one oyster after another, the heat of passion spread to her neck and throat. He saw.

Abruptly, she wrenched her eyes from his gaze and hurried away. With a brief apology to Mary for leaving the party so soon, she retired to her bedroom.

Frances had never felt so disconsolate. She had always thought of herself as self-possessed; now she felt possessed by a confusion of feelings which she had never experienced before: rage, passion, humiliation, desire, the need for attention. She had always thought of herself as clear-sighted and confident in all her actions; now she felt confused and uncertain what the future might hold. Gradually she came to understand that she had changed, that her life would now be different, that she would be different.

So, she began to wonder how she might allow full expression of these new feelings yet remain true to being her own woman. She felt such passion, and such fury with the man for treating her with disdain whilst inflaming her desire. She pondered how to make him meet her with equal passion, fury and desire. How to get his attention! How to make him prove his mettle as the man for her. As a plan formed, a wicked and determined smile enlivened her face and lifted her spirits.

The following day, Benjamin was at his lodgings enjoying an early breakfast, with a tub of fresh oysters at hand, when he received an unexpected visit from Mary's husband, William, delivering a letter addressed to 'Benjamin Child' under a plain seal. Benjamin broke the seal with his oyster knife and read: 'I challenge you to a duel to the death tomorrow morning at dawn in Calcot Woods. I shall supply weapons. Signed, Nemesis.'

Benjamin was bemused. He wondered whom he could have offended, and how, for he was a stranger here, knowing no one beyond his old friend William and his new wife. Who could this

Nemesis be? William proffered no explanation, but offered to stand as Benjamin's second for the duel. Benjamin's enjoyment of his breakfast oysters was ruined.

His day was ruined. He knew he was an able swordsman, but fretted as to whom his adversary might be. He had been enjoying a leisurely breakfast, revisiting the previous evening's encounter with the unknown woman as he prised open his matutinal oysters, relishing the memory of the rising passion at her throat and neck, wondering how he might discover her. Now these pleasant thoughts splintered into a cascade of compelling anxieties – uncertainty, fear, distress, incomprehension – his mind a cavalcade of confused and compulsive thoughts.

After a troubled, sleepless night, Benjamin donned his linen shirt, loose doublet and breeches, and a cocked hat, and rode to Calcot Woods, then groped his way anxiously into the trees, with William following. In the dawn light, Benjamin saw two strange young men approaching. They looked slim and fit. They wore tight, black doublets and breeches and cocked hats, their faces partly covered by half masks above beardless chins. The shorter of the two carried a long box which Benjamin took to contain their duelling weapons. As the young men drew closer, Benjamin's anxieties grew stronger and stronger – confusion, threat, weakness, a sense of unreality, of being not in control of events – nothing which might help him defend his life.

The young second opened the box of weapons, which lay in a bed of green baize. Benjamin saw a brace of Berkshire backswords, the long wooden kind with basket hilts that yokels use in their revels, with which they fight and break heads. As a skilled swordsman, Benjamin felt the indignity of being offered practice weapons to fight a duel. But, the sight of the masked young men bearing such weapons left Benjamin amazed and dismayed, deepening his sense of unreality, and he was unable to protest.

Offering Benjamin his choice of Berkshire backsword, the young second declared to the woods in a deep booming voice, 'We shall begin with a brief trial bout for the combatants to warm up and become familiar with their weapons before we strip and commence the duel in earnest. At my signal!'

The bout commenced; slash, blow, feint, parry. Benjamin's confidence grew with each stroke as he was lured into thinking he was getting the measure of his adversary. His right wrist was strong and pliant after straining against so much oyster muscle; he thought he could feint for a low strike against his opponent's right leg, to make him draw down his sword, then with a quick flick of the wrist he could direct a savage blow powerful enough to smash his adversary's right arm. The blow was quick, but his adversary's flick was quicker. By the time the blow struck, the full length of his opponent's arm was protected by the firmly gripped backsword. Instead of delivering a blow against soft tissue, Benjamin's backsword was brought short against the tough cudgel, jarring his shoulder and throwing him off balance.

His antagonist took the opportunity to strike for Benjamin's head, setting his cocked hat askew and leaving a weal above his left temple; just a tap it was, but still painful. Then Benjamin heard the half circle swish of the backsword before it caught the back of his knees and brought him to the ground. Now, the backsword was pressing against his neck behind his right ear, forcing him down further. The bout was over.

Stepping away, his tormentor's arms reached backwards to allow the second to pull off the doublet in a single movement, revealing the binding about the chest beneath her linen shirt. Frances tore off the cocked hat with one hand and the half mask, left over from a masked ball, with the other. As she shook out her plait, her auburn hair cascaded over her shoulders. Setting her arms akimbo, Frances leaned forward towards her prostrate adversary. As he lifted his eyes, she met and held his gaze and treated him to her most beatific and triumphant smile.

He was distraught. She had manipulated him, tricked him, wounded him, overcome him in combat. He felt utterly humiliated. He was wrong. Only when his friend Mary removed her disguise and he saw that she had been witness to his ignominy was his humiliation complete. Nemesis! Then a burning rage ignited in his cheeks and neck at the humiliation to which this woman, who still held his gaze, had subjected him. He slowly rose to his feet, lifting his backsword from the ground. His lips curled back in an angry grimace, and he prepared to raise his cudgel and stand his ground for further affray.

Frances laughed, waving her backsword before his face. Now, she thought with a giggle, I have his attention.

'Well, Sire,' she said, 'have a duel with me. We can be in earnest now if you so wish. It will bring you no disgrace. But, you have another choice, which will bring you no disgrace neither. You can fight me or you can wed me. This is your choice. So, what are you to do? Fight me or wed me!'

He felt bewildered, flummoxed and nonplussed at this further rapid twist in this woman's supple wits. He gazed at her, leaning towards him with arms akimbo, her auburn hair falling forward about a face warm with the passion of combat, mischief, mirth and – now he saw it – desire. From his humiliation and rage there blossomed his own bright passion. His face relaxed. He grinned back at her. Holding her gaze, he painfully dropped to one knee, 'Well,' he said, 'this is a difficult dilemma, hard to choose, yet, on balance, I feel, yes, wedding you has the edge.'

He rose and they swiftly fell into each other's arms, just as swiftly leapt onto their horses, and galloped over the fields, leaping the hedges and ditches till they reached Wargrave Rectory. They beat urgently upon the door until the rector appeared in nightshirt and nightcap. By the time he was dressed in his priestly garb, and (as he firmly insisted) breakfasted, Mary and William had arrived at a less urgent pace befitting a married couple, to act now not as seconds but as witnesses. And so, the joining in marriage of Frances Kendrick and Benjamin Child was celebrated with great rejoicing.

SOURCE

Anonymous poem, 'The Berkshire Lady's Garland'

❧

The marriage of Frances Kendrick and Benjamin Child was celebrated and duly registered at St Mary's Church, Wargrave, on 28 March 1707.

TWENTY SEVEN

RETURN TO READING

We continued through Tilehurst, an area which produces much of the materials for Reading's famous red, cream and grey brickwork which patterns the local buildings. Proceeding into the town, we returned to our original meeting place, the Great Western Hotel. We left the wagonette for the last time, patting goodbye to our horses, and walked east to the Forbury Gardens and the abbey ruins beyond. Here, at the end of our journey, we heard Harold Benjamin tell the last part of the Trial by Combat of Henry de Essex and Robert de Montfort:

TRIAL BY COMBAT (2) –
THE RECKONING AND THE REDEMPTION

Judgement of the King's Court at Windsor
Now, all the strands of Henry de Essex's villainous life have converged: the discrediting of Robert de Vere, the treachery at Ewloe, the defrauding of St Edmund, and the merciless usage of Gilbert de Cereville. Yet, Henry de Essex feels neither compassion towards those whom he has ill-used nor remorse for his misdeeds. All his thoughts centre upon his self-justification, the ingratitude of his king, and how he will prove the rightness of his cause by slaughtering his adversary.

❧

When the savage torture and killing of innocent Gilbert de Cereville by de Essex became known, even cynical Norman

❧

nobles were shocked by such extreme behaviour. This was now the time for the coiled viper in Robert de Montfort's vitals to strike.

At the King's Court at Windsor Castle, Robert formally accused de Essex of treason during the Battle of Ewloe. The ruling of the court was for Henry de Essex to face a Trial by Combat. By this judicial ordeal, God's judgement on de Essex's guilt or innocence was to be discovered: if he died, then he was guilty; if he prevailed then he was innocent in the sight of God. To prove de Essex's guilt by his own body, Robert put himself forward as de Essex's adversary in the ordeal.

Trial by Combat

Henry de Essex watches from the edge of the field as the common people, monks and clerics, soldiers and trumpeters, servants and retainers, gentry and nobility, gradually gather in the spring sunlight, eager to enjoy the sport.

Common people crowd together, jostling and jocular, on the south bank of the silver streaming Thames. Corpulent clerics and lean Cluniac monks cluster around Abbot Roger's dais. Richly bedecked and bejewelled nobles gather around King Henry's dais. Retainers busy themselves in the pavilions, laying out the arms and armour, colours and crests for their masters, burnishing their breastplates.

All around the field there is feasting and quaffing, light-hearted banter and gaiety, merriment and growing excitement. Yet, dominating the scene is the monastery founded by King Henry Beauclerc; from its dark walls and grim towers it keeps solemn watch over the proceedings below.

Henry de Essex watches as Robert de Montfort steps from his pavilion, yawning and stretching, looking fit and strong, ready for battle. The two men gaze at one another across the field, their eyes dark with loathing, and then they turn away and enter their pavilions.

With a blare of trumpets, Abbot Roger's barge approaches the eyot's northern shore. He is greeted by a crowd of black-cloaked Cluniac monks, scurrying about and waving their arms like a flock of cormorants, as they lead him to his dais. Shortly after, another blare of trumpets, and the royal barge slides into its moorage. Soldiers gather around the King for protection as he processes across the field in splendour, with his nobles pushing and shoving to be closest to him, as he takes his place on the dais beneath the scarlet and orange canopy.

Henry de Essex and Robert de Montfort, armed cap à pie *– covered from head to foot in glittering armour – clump from their pavilions. Robert wears a surcoat and carries a triangular bowed shield, each in his colours of yellow and blue stripes. de Essex's surcoat and shield are white with a scarlet zig-zag. As the combatants make obeisance to their sovereign, a deep hush falls over the field, and at his signal the two men raise their swords and combat is joined.*

There is no subtlety about this test of endurance and hardihood. The opponents slug it out, their swords clanking loudly on shield and crested helm and heavy armour. They butt one another like rams, they wrestle and thump, they try to knock one another over, they reel from the dizzying blows. The crowd on the shore shout and jeer and curse, with cat-calls and coarse chants; the Cluniacs close their ears. The slugging goes on for a long time. The crowd becomes bored and restless, some drift away, to be joshed and taunted for ever after for what they were to miss.

Robert reels back from a ringing blow to his helm. de Essex, moving to take advantage of his opponent's vertigo, is stopped in his lumbering tracks: dominating the southern sky he sees a doleful vision – St Edmund, glorious king and martyr, his body pierced by dark heathen shafts, and about his crowned and sainted head bright shafts of radiant light. St Edmund looks towards de Essex with a severe countenance.

Beside him, Gilbert de Cereville, gaunt and emaciated, casts vengeful looks upon his tormentor. St Edmund and Gilbert point accusing fingers at Henry de Essex, calling down dire imprecations on his head for all his dread misdeeds.

The vision holds Henry de Essex transfixed. He had taken pride in himself as an ambitious, vicious, ruthless man without remorse or moral scruple. Now, the full weight of his crimes presses upon his soul – the discrediting of de Vere, the treachery at Ewloe, the defrauding of St Edmund, the merciless usage of Gilbert de Cereville. In that moment of insight, the internal conflict in Henry's soul becomes one with the external conflict on the field. Raging against the feelings of guilt, remorse and shame which rise in his breast, he focuses the full fury of his wrath upon his adversary.

Casting aside his shield, de Essex grasps his sword in both hands and attacks Robert with a wild frenzy, as if to beat down his defences by sheer force. The crowd is suddenly alert at this turn of the battle, screaming and groaning at every savage stroke. Robert warily retreats from this onslaught, avoiding the weighty blows, or taking them on his shield, or side-stepping and allowing the momentum of the blow to carry through, exposing de Essex's side and shoulder to a telling counter-stroke.

The effort of his surge of violent ire, Robert's defensive play, and the many wounds to his undefended flanks, drain and exhaust de Essex. With de Essex at his mercy, Robert briskly inflicts a coup de grâce *and steps back. Henry de Essex stands motionless. His sword slips from his hands. His arms reach out towards the vision of St Edmund and Gilbert. Then his eyes glaze over. He begins to topple forward like a felled tree, with slow descent, arms outspread, burnished breastplate bright in the sun as it crashes onto the field. A deep hush settles again upon the crowd. All is still.*

Redemption of Henry de Essex

Then, Cluniac monks flock forward, roll Henry's body onto a waiting bier, and in slow and solemn procession they carry him from the field, followed by Abbot Roger and his brethren, the King and his nobles, and the victorious Robert de Montfort. They cross the river by barge, wind their way into the monastery by the River Gate, and deposit their burden with the infirmarian.

The infirmarian carefully removes Henry's armour to prepare his body for burial, only to find him alive, though grievously wounded and close to death. The infirmarian gently dresses Henry's wounds with healing salves from the monastery's herb garden, gives him water to drink, and sits by his pallet by day and night until full consciousness returns.

Meanwhile, the King rules that Henry de Essex is guilty of his crimes in the sight of God. All his fiefs and fortune are forfeit to the Crown and afforded to Robert de Montfort for his bravery in the Trial by Combat.

Amidst the peaceful surroundings of the infirmary, and under the patient care of the infirmarian, Henry's wounds gradually heal. When sufficiently recovered, he is clothed in the habit and cowl of a monk and entrusted to the master of the novices, who teaches him the practices of the religious life of prayer and service. At the end of his novitiate, a day is appointed for him to take his vows; in this solemn ceremony the candidate receives the kiss of peace as a token of his reception into the full charity of the Cluniac brotherhood.

The man who once served the King as Constable and Standard Bearer spends the rest of his days serving the poor, the pilgrim, the leper, the sick, and the dying, atoning for his previous vicious life and transforming his life into virtue.

෴

Uplifted by our final tale, we bade each other a hearty farewell and went our several ways.

Sources

Hurry, Jamieson B., *The Trial by Combat of Henry de Essex and Robert de Montfort at Reading Abbey*, 1919

Childs, W.M., *The Story of the Town of Reading*, 1905

෴

The events in the story are based on Jamieson Hurry's book and Harry Morley's painting. However, although this story includes some historical events, it is not a history. Yet, it is more than a folk tale. It is a powerful, spiritual story about the redemption of a wicked life. The turning point in Henry de Essex's life is the vision of St Edmund in the Radingian sky.

GLOSSARY

ANGLO-SAXON	ENGLISH
Æthelingaeg	Athelney
Assedone	Ashdown
Basengum	Basing
Bearrucscir	Berkshire
Cippanhamm	Chippenham
Ethandun	Eddington
Fearndun	Faringdon
fyrd	Anglo-Saxon militia
Gleawecestre	Gloucester
Hamtunscir	Hampshire
Hingefelda	Englefield
Hungreford	Hungerford
Mertone	Merton
Norphymbre	Northumbria
Offentona	Uffington
Readingum	Reading
Snotengaham	Nottingham
Sumorsæte	Somerset
Temes	Thames
Waneting	Wantage
Wiltunscir	Wiltshire

BIBLIOGRAPHY

Books

Barham, Revd Richard H. (pen name Thomas Ingoldsby Esquire), *The Ingoldsby Legends*, Richard Bentley & Sons, 1894

Briggs, Katharine M., *A Dictionary of British Folk-Tales in the English Language*, Indiana University Press, 1971

Child, Francis James, *The English and Scottish Popular Ballads*, Vol. 5, Courier Dover Publications, 2003

Childs, W.M., *The Story of the Town of Reading*, Reading, Long, 1905

Crossley-Holland, Kevin, *The Norse Myths*, Andre Deutsch, 1980

Dearmer, Percy, *The Little Lives of the Saints*, Wells Gardner, Darton & Co., 1900

Deloney, Thomas, *The History of Thomas of Reading; Or, the Six Worthy Yeomen of the West*, Eliz. Allde for Robert Bird, 1632

Ditchfield, P.H. (Ed.), *Bygone Berkshire*, EP Publishing Ltd British Book Centre, 1975

Ekwall, Eilert, *Concise Oxford Dictionary of English Place-Names*, The Clarendon Press, 1960

Fitch, Eric, *In Search of Herne the Hunter*, Capall Bann Publishing, 1994

Fuller, Thomas, *The History of the Worthies of England*, Thomas Williams, 1662

Gray, Edward William, *The History and Antiquities of Newbury and its Environs*, 1839

Gray, Rosemary (Ed.), *The Book of Wargrave*, Wargrave Local History Society, *c.* 1986

Hammond, Nigel, *Rural Life in the Vale of the White Horse 1780-1914*, William Smith (Booksellers) Ltd, 1997

Hartsiotis, Kirsty, *Wiltshire Folk Tales*, The History Press, 2011

Hibbert, Christopher, *The Court at Windsor: A Domestic History*, Longmans, 1964

Huntley, Elsie, *Boxford Barleycorn*, Abbey Press, 1970

Hurry, Jamieson B., *The Trial by Combat of Henry de Essex and Robert de Montfort at Reading Abbey*, Elliot Stock, 1919

Kerry, Charles, *History and Antiquities of the Hundred of Bray*, Savill and Edwards, 1861

Lee, Sidney (Ed.), *Dictionary of National Biography*, Vol. LVII, Smith, Elder & Co., 1899

Liddell Hart, Basil, *History of the First World War*, Pan Books Ltd, 1972

Lowsley, Major B., *Berkshire Words and Phrases*, Trübner & Co., 1888

Marsh, W. H., *Illustrated Guide to Maidenhead and the Surrounding Country*, W.H. Marsh (late Richards), 1896

Mitford, Mary Russell, *Our Village: Sketches of Rural Character and Scenery* (first appearing in *The Lady's Magazine*, 1820s and 1830s)

Money, Walter, *The History of the Ancient Town and Borough of Newbury in the County of Berkshire*, Parker and Co., 1887

Morris, W.A.D., *A History of the Parish of Shaw-cum-Donnington*, Newbury, 1969

Read, William, *John Francis Dandridge, Machine Breaker or Swing Rioter*, Self-published, 2010

Rosen, Barbara (Ed.), *Witchcraft in England: 1558-1618*, The University of Massachusetts Press, 1991

Salmon, Miss L., *Untravelled Berkshire*, Sampson Low, 1909

Sharpe, Frederick, *The Church Bells of Berkshire*, Kingsmead Reprints, 1970

Simpson, Jacqueline and Roud, Steve, *A Dictionary of English Folklore*, Oxford University Press, 2000

Slater, Gilbert, *The English Peasantry and the Enclosure of Common Fields*, Archibald Constable & Co. Ltd, 1907

Stephen, Leslie (Ed.), *Dictionary of National Biography*, Vol. XVI, Smith, Elder & Co., 1888

Summers, Revd W.H. and Peake, Harold (Eds), *The Story of Hungerford in Berkshire*, The Trustees of the Borough and Manor of Hungerford, 1926

Taylor, Paul B. and Auden, W.H., 'The Lay of Volund', in *The Elder Edda*, Faber and Faber, 1969

Verney, Margaret M., *Bucks Biographies: A School Book*, The Clarendon Press, 1912

Viles, Edward, *Black Bess; Or the Knight of the Road*, E. Harrison, 1866

Vincent, James Edmund, *Highways and Byways of Berkshire*, Macmillan, 1906

Vinycomb, John, *Fictitious and Symbolic Creatures in Art*, Chapman and Hall, 1906

Westwood, Jennifer and Simpson, Jacqueline, *The Lore of the Land*, Penguin, 2006

Williams, Alfred, *Round About the Upper Thames*, Duckworth & Co., 1915; Nabu Press, 2010

Williams, Alfred, *Villages of the White Horse*, Duckworth & Co., 1913; The History Press, 2007

NEWSPAPERS, JOURNALS AND ARTICLES

Berkshire Mercury, 27 April 1972; 6 October 1977

Chambers, Jill, 'Berkshire machine breakers – Captain Swing and the 1830 riots', *Berkshire Family Historian*, Vol. 23, No. 3, March 2000

Kirkwood, Jean, 'The Windsor Martyrs – Burnt at the Stake', *Windlesora*, No. 27, Windsor Local History Group, 2011

Kupfermann, Elias, 'A Case of Witchcraft in Elizabethan Windsor', *Windlesora*, No. 27, Windsor Local History Group, 2011

Reading Evening Post, 30 October 1969

Reading Mercury, November to December 1830; 22 September 1956; 23 September 1961

PAMPHLETS

Alde, John, 'A brief treatyse conteyninge the most strange and horrible crueltye of Elizabeth Sule alias Bockingham and hir confederates, executed at Abington, upon Richard Galis' [*sic*], Bodleian Library Reference: 'Gough Berks. I', 1579

White, Edward, 'A rehearsal both straung and true of hainous and horrible actes committed by Elizabeth Style, Alias Rockingham, Mother Dutten, Mother Devell, Mother Margaret, Fower notorious witches, apprehended at Winsore in the Countie of Barks, and at Abington arraigned, condemned and executed On the 28th daye of February laste, Anno. 1579', British Library Reference: c.27.a.11, 1579

POEMS

Anonymous, 'The Berkshire Lady's Garland' (can be sung to the tune of 'The Royal Forester')

OTHER

Berkshire Local History Committee, Berkshire Records

Berkshire Local History Library, Collection of Berkshire Mummers Plays and Fragments of Traditional Rhymes

Goodchild, W., 'Fragments of Local Legends and History', a paper read before the Wellington College Natural Science Society, 9 February 1878

Heelas, Arthur T., 'Historical Sketch of Wokingham', a lecture given by Arthur T. Heelas, 1930

Matthews, Tony, *The Witches of Windsor: A Community Play*, performed as part of the Windsor Arts Scene in November 2011, unpublished

Proceedings of Societies, Newbury and District Field Club, Excursion to Tom Hughes' Country – Uffington, Kingston Lisle, White Horse Hill, Waylen Smith's Cave, Donnington Priory, 1912

ENDNOTES

1. The title of Edward Viles' penny dreadful, published in 1866 with a colourful cover.
2. *Encomium Emmae Reginae.*
3. Political spin is not just a modern phenomenon.
4. The three main articles of belief were Transubstantiation, receiving Communion by bread alone being sufficient for salvation, and a celibate priesthood.
5. St John's Wort.
6. From 'Greensleeves'.
7. This pub was demolished to make way for Bracknell & Wokingham College.
8. Francis Bacon, 1st Viscount St Albans, Attorney General and Lord Chancellor of England.
9. Ladywell, Speen.
10. 'The "white witch", wise woman or Cunning Man, often believed in his powers as inborn and took pride in them.' Rosen, Barbara, 1991.
11. A gallon loaf had a weight of 8lb 11oz, or 3.94kg.
12. St Luke's Gospel, Chapter 15, Verse 4.
13. St John's Gospel, Chapter 10, Verse 11.
14. Bats and tawny owls.
15. A backsword is a basket-hilted slashing sword which has one sharpened edge and a flat 'back' or 'spine' on its unsharpened edge. The practice sword version of the backsword is made from a 3ft length of ash with a basket hilt.

INDEX

If you enjoyed this book, you may also be interested in…

Sussex Folk Tales

MICHAEL O'LEARY

From ghosts and madmen to witches and wise women, Michael O'Leary reveals many of the hidden horrors of Sussex – horrors that can be foun in the most beautiful places, or that lurk beneath the seemingly mundane. Sussex Folk Tales takes t reader beyond the written page and shows them the wonders that lie within the Sussex landscape.

978 0 7524 7469 4

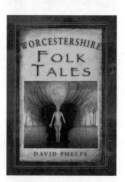

Worcestershire Folk Tales

DAVID PHELPS

From battles of the Civil War to witchcraft trials, Worcestershire is steeped in history – and almost every village has some dark tale of magical event tell. Even the holy community is not safe – veng ance, infidelity and murder loom large in the cou ty's religious history. Complemented by beautiful illustrations, Worcestershire Folk Tales is crammee with these myths, legends and mysterious yarns.

978 0 7524 8580 5

Haunted Berkshire

ROGER LONG

For such a small county, reports of supernatural happenings around Berkshire are surprisingly plentiful and varied. The haunting figures range from shades of kings, queens and dukes to sobbin maidens and moaning men. They haunt all mann of places such as castles, mansions, churchyards, cottages, follies and grottoes. So read on to see w goes bump in the Berkshire night.

978 0 7524 5907 3

Visit our website and discover thousands of other History Press books.

www.thehistorypress.co.uk